The Flying Bishop
The Life of the Rt Revd J R 'Jack' Weller
Bishop in South America 1934–1946

The Flying Bishop
*The Life of the Rt Revd J R 'Jack' Weller
Bishop in South America 1934–1946*

John Weller

ATHENA PRESS
LONDON

The Flying Bishop
Copyright © John Weller 2008

All Rights Reserved

No part of this book may be reproduced in any form
by photocopying or by any electronic or mechanical means,
including information storage or retrieval systems,
without permission in writing from both the copyright
owner and the publisher of this book.

ISBN 978 1 84748 225 9

First Published 2008 by
ATHENA PRESS
Queen's House, 2 Holly Road
Twickenham TW1 4EG
United Kingdom

Printed for Athena Press

The Rt Revd J R 'Jack' Weller

Foreword

By the end of the twentieth century, there were seventeen Anglican dioceses in South America, each presided over by its bishop. It is an indication of how the church has expanded that as recently as the 1940s there were only two dioceses covering the same area; these were presided over by just one bishop who was responsible for all Anglican work between the Panama Canal and the island of South Georgia in the Antarctic.

It required someone with an unusual combination of qualities to perform this task successfully. Besides, like all bishops, having the spirituality and the preaching, teaching and administrative ability to perform the functions of that office, he needed to be physically strong enough to manage the enormous amount of travelling, by all sorts of means, such a huge diocese required (and, incidentally, he needed also to pay for the travelling out of his own pocket; at the time of his appointment, the Archbishop of Canterbury warned him that there was no travel allowance available). He also needed to be experienced, having encountered all kinds of people of many races and cultures in the past, as he would certainly be required to do so in the future.

It can reasonably be claimed that the bishop who held the post in the years up to 1946 did indeed have all these qualities, and was thus able to play his part in laying the foundations for the enormous expansion which was to follow. This is the story of Jack Weller's life.

Contents

Background and Boyhood 1880–1898	11
Ceylon, South Africa and North America 1898–1907	15
Vocation and Ordination 1907–1913	18
The Middle East and Marriage 1913–1920	21
Missions to Seamen 1920–1934	25
Bereavement and Consecration 1934	30
Journey to the Falklands I 1934	32
Journey to the Falklands II 1934–1935	36
South Georgia, Argentina and the North 1935–1936	39
'The Flying Bishop' 1936	43
Extra Responsibility and Breakdown 1936–1938	47
Marriage and Return to the Diocese 1938	52
An Ordination and an Earthquake in Chile 1938–1939	56
Chaco Mission and Synod 1939	60
Journey to Panama I 1939–1940	64
Journey to Panama II 1940	67
Fatherhood and Synod 1940–1942	70
Araucania, the North-West and Chaco 1942–1943	74
Last Years in the Diocese 1943–1946	78

Edwalton and Holme Pierrepont 1946–1958	81
The Final Years 1958–1969	86
A Note on Sources	88
Map of South America	90
Family Tree	91
Index	93

Background and Boyhood 1880–98

On 10 December, 1872, there occurred an event at Chesham in Buckinghamshire which, the local newspaper informs us, caused a considerable stir in the town. This was the double wedding of the two daughters of the late vicar, the Revd Adolphus Frederick Aylward. The church was full to overflowing an hour before the service began, with hundreds unable to gain admittance.[1]

Mr Aylward had been appointed to the post at the young age of twenty-five, and, during his incumbency, two more churches were built in the parish, and Chesham's ancient church restored. Then in 1871 there occurred a typhus epidemic. The vicar visited the sick assiduously, although 'all classes of people tried their utmost to keep him from visiting the stricken poor'.[2] He contracted the disease himself, and died at the age of fifty. A brass memorial in St Mary's Church, erected by 'the poor of Chesham', expresses their appreciation of his devoted ministry. His widow and daughters remained in the town, and now, just a year after their father's death, the daughters were married together. The younger one, Edith Emma, married Edward Weller from the neighbouring town of Amersham.

The Weller family had farmed in Oxfordshire for at least 250 years, but in the middle of the eighteenth century a young member of the family, William, moved to High Wycombe in Buckinghamshire; in 1758, he married a local woman named Ann House. In 1771 he acquired a brewery in nearby Amersham, and subsequent generations expanded the business so that it became a major employer in the town. By the year of the double wedding, the business had been inherited by three of William's great-grandsons: William, who was not involved in actually running it; Edward, who at twenty-nine years of age was responsible for the farms and other property; and George, who looked after the

---

[1] The *Buckinghamshire Advertiser*, 14 Dec, 1872.
[2] The *Bucks Examiner*, 21 Nov, 1930.

brewery itself. To enable the farm workers to celebrate their employer's marriage, a meal was provided in Amersham, with 'an unlimited supply of malt liquor' for no less than seventy of them, which indicates that Edward's responsibilities were considerable.[3]

Edward and Edith settled in a house in Amersham, and before long were the parents of three sons and three daughters. This necessitated a move to a larger property, so in 1879 they moved to Blackwell Hall, three miles from Amersham. Here four more sons were born, the eldest of them on 6 October 1880. He was christened John Reginald. John was a name held by many members of the family, including a brother and an uncle of the child's father, but in fact the boy came to be known as Jack.

Blackwell Hall was the family's home for the next ten years. It is a delightful house with extensive grounds and stables where the carriage horses and Edward's hunters were kept, which were a great source of attraction for the children. Jack was destined to do an enormous amount of travelling in adult life, but his first journeys in those days before there were cars and tarred roads were in a three-wheeled pram, then in a carriage drawn by two goats, then on a donkey called Neddy, and later on a pony.[4]

Discipline was strict, with corporal punishment often used to ensure good behaviour, but Jack had many happy memories of his boyhood. Education was provided by a nursery governess, whose task must have been a difficult one, since the children were at various stages of development, but after a time the eldest three children were sent to a school in Brighton.

Life at Blackwell Hall came to an end in 1889, when it was felt that the educational needs of the younger members of the family required that all of them should move to the seaside town where the elder ones were already at school. This meant that Edward had to divide his time between his home in Brighton and the care of the property in Amersham. The frequent travelling may have undermined his health, for he died of pneumonia a year after the move, at the age of forty-six. Edith was thus left with the task of caring for ten children, ranging in age from sixteen and a half to two and a half.

---

[3] Ibid.
[4] Weller, J R, *Bishop over the Andes*, unpublished.

The task might have been too much for an ordinary woman, but Edith was not an ordinary woman. This is what her son Christopher wrote about the person who had such a strong influence not only on him, but also on Jack and their siblings:

> From the moment her husband died she just gave herself to meet the needs of her children. A less brave woman would have been daunted by the task. 'Mother' was never daunted. A deeply religious woman, she met every difficulty (and there were plenty of difficulties during the next thirty years) with a calm serenity which never faltered. Her motto was 'live one day at a time'. Her method: an ever-growing reliance on God. Seldom during those years was there adequate domestic help. Always only just sufficient income to pay the expenses of educating her large family [...] Upon her gravestone are carved words she uttered more than once in her last hours: 'O Lord, in thee have I trusted'. That phrase from the 'Te Deum' gives the secret of her life – devout, unshakable trust in God. Perhaps the fact which gave her the greatest happiness in her latter years was that she had lived to see four of her sons enter the ministry of the Church of which she was such a devoted member.[5]

In 1894, the family moved again. Bedford was felt to have educational advantages, and Christopher, Jack and their three younger brothers all went to Bedford Grammar School (now Bedford School); it was a school with an excellent reputation under a remarkable headmaster, Surtees Philpotts. Jack developed in many ways during the next few years, not only educationally, but physically; he was good at games and an excellent swimmer.

As Jack neared the end of his time at school, he considered possible careers. His ambition had for some time been to serve in the Navy; he was known even before his father's death as 'Father's sailor boy'. He went to London to apply to serve on the *Britannia*, and encountered the first great disappointment of his life when he was turned down because of defective eyesight – a decision which to the end of his days he felt to be based on the oculist's error.[6]

---

[5] Weller, C H, *A Few Notes Concerning the Edward Wellers*, unpublished.
[6] Weller, J R, *Bishop over the Andes*.

He returned to school, where one of the masters suggested that he might qualify as a naval engineer. He studied the relevant subjects, but a further disappointment occurred when, although he passed the examinations in all the other subjects, he failed in one which at that time was essential: German.

One of Jack's godfathers was his uncle William, who had in fact paid the fees for his education at Bedford School. William suggested banking as a possible career, and arranged an interview with a distinguished member of that profession from South Africa, who duly offered him a post. To his uncle's displeasure, Jack turned it down because, in his words, 'my ideas about life did not include that of spending most of it sitting on my rump.'[7]

However, a few days later, Jack met a tea-planter from Ceylon (now Sri Lanka), whose description of life out there sounded much more attractive than banking in South Africa. When Jack expressed interest, the tea-planter said he had a brother who would employ him and train him for a consideration of £100. To his credit, Jack's uncle William provided the money, and on 5 February 1898, at the age of seventeen and a half, Jack boarded a ship in Southampton bound for Colombo, and thus began his travels.

---

[7] Ibid.

Ceylon, South Africa and North America 1898–1907

The tea estate where Jack was to work was in a remote part of the country. He lived with his employer, a Mr Laurie, and worked hard on the estate, as well as trying to learn the local language. The Laurie family were very devout, with daily prayers as well as Sunday worship, but after six months there was a change in Jack's life. He was approached about a job with another tea estates company and decided to accept. He now had a small bungalow of his own, and he had as neighbours many other young men, employed on the various estates. He found that when he went to church, he was the only man who stayed behind for the Communion part of the Sunday service, and that the reason for this was that 'the opportunities for satisfying the lusts of the flesh were many; some young men kept native women, and most of them drank a great deal too much whisky.'[1] What happened next is also best described in Jack's own words:

> I played a fairly good game of rugger and played for the Up-Country team, which brought me into still closer contact with the young men in the island. Soon I began to look on life with their eyes, to join in anything that was going, and to realise that in the East 'there were no Ten Commandments'. We had weekend parties at one another's bungalows, and as long as we did our work well, the bosses did not seem to mind what we did in our leisure. The standard of life drifted farther and farther from that to which I had been raised. Life became very expensive, debts began to mount. I began to make mistakes in my work, and could no longer stand the pace set by my companions. I came to the conclusion that it would be better for me to return home, and my boss agreed.[2]

---

[1] Weller, J R, *Bishop over the Andes*.
[2] Ibid.

Ceylon, South Africa and North America 1898–1907

The Boer War was now in progress, so on his return to England, Jack volunteered for military service and was enrolled in the 32nd battalion of the Imperial Yeomanry[3], serving in the ranks of a unit consisting almost entirely of lads from Lancashire. They trained at the Wellington Barracks in Aldershot, and the strict discipline and hard physical activity were just what Jack needed after the last part of his stay in Ceylon.

The battalion was sent to Cape Town in 1901 and camped near Stellenbosch. There were plenty of opportunities for sport, as well as much moving about in Cape Colony in mud and rain. Meanwhile the war finished without Jack's unit seeing any action, and they returned to England. Jack remarked that the journeys in troopships to and from South Africa were 'quite an education, and I learned to mix with all kinds of men in very close quarters'[4] On landing he was discharged from the army, and warmly welcomed by the family.

On considering what to do next, Jack found that many people were migrating to Canada, so he decided to do the same, and for the first time he crossed the Atlantic; the liner in which he travelled from Liverpool took nineteen days to reach St John, New Brunswick, encountering storms and fog on the way. One of his elder brothers, Morton, had migrated some years before, and Jack found a job on a farm belonging to relatives of Morton's wife. He soon learnt to chop trees, milk cows, plough and make maple sugar. He then learnt that wages were better across the border in the United States, so he transferred to a farm in Maine, where the main crop was potatoes. He also looked after horses, and worked as a lumberjack in winter, becoming proficient with an axe.

This was the beginning of a six-year period in which Jack, having 'caught the wandering fever', travelled very widely in the United States, doing a large variety of temporary jobs. He had a number of adventures. On one occasion he decided to visit England by working his way on a cattle ship. He got into an argument with a Mexican of mixed race, who tried to kill him, first with a pitchfork, then with a knife. Jack was strong and

---

[3] Weller, *A Few Notes Concerning the Edward Wellers*
[4] Weller, J R, *Bishop over the Andes*

repelled both attacks, though receiving a knife wound on his arm. Fortunately, before the voyage, he had taken pity on two cattle-hands who looked undernourished, and had stood them a meal. They repaid him by watching over him at night, in case the Mexican tried to attack him in his sleep.[5]

On another occasion, in Chicago, Jack was attacked in the street by two confidence tricksters, who were enraged when Jack refused to believe their story. He had the sense to wait until they were in a public place before he told them this. He was told by the manager of the hotel where he was staying that the men were members of a very dangerous gang, and that Jack was lucky to be alive. He decided he had had enough of Chicago, and took a train to Concord, New Hampshire, where he had a friend named George Shaw who was working on the Boston and Maine Railroad. Jack accepted a job in the Locomotive Department, which involved yet another new trade for him: repairing locomotives. He had, however, taken an engineering course while at school, so most of the tools were familiar to him. He stayed with his friend, who lived about four miles from the workshops, and who drove him to and from work in a one-horse buggy. Work finished at five, giving him ample time to think about where his life was going, and this had important results.[6]

---

[5] Ibid.
[6] Ibid.

Vocation and Ordination 1907–1913

Jack has given his own account of the turning point in his life. This is what he wrote:

> This blessed leisure gave me more time for thought, or perhaps I had come to the period in a man's life when he is apt to think more seriously. My mind turned towards religion, and I decided to find out for myself the truth about those things I had been taught about God. My adult life had not been an evil one, but it had been a careless one, with no serious thought about the whys and wherefores of life. I told George Shaw that I proposed going to church. He would not accompany me, as I chose the American Episcopal (Anglican) Church. He explained that he would not be wanted among all the grand people who attended that Church; he would be much more at home in the Methodist Church, or at the Salvation Army.
>
> It was some years since I had attended Church, and as the familiar service made some sort of sentimental appeal, I decided to do so again. Thus, for three Sundays in October, 1907, I attended Church and began to realise that there was a great deal more in life than work and careless pleasure. Still, I wanted earnestly to test the value of the ministrations of the Church, and having made a more careful preparation before Holy Communion than ever before, I attended that service on the early morning of All Saints Day, which fell on a Sunday.
>
> This was to change the entire course of my life, for as I knelt at the altar rails, I became conscious of the reality of Jesus, and life became filled with a new purpose – to attempt to help other people to realise that the message the Apostles proclaimed after the Ascension is true; that Jesus lives.'[1]

Jack continued to worship in the church, St Paul's, Concord, on Sundays, and when he heard that there was a special Communion service on St Andrew's Day at the end of the month, for members

---

[1] Weller, J R, *Bishop over the Andes*

of a men's group called the St Andrew's Fellowship, he excused himself from work (the day fell on a Thursday) in order to be present.

The Rector of St Paul's, the Revd Stanley Emery, had only recently been appointed to the parish. He had noticed Jack, and made enquiries of members of the congregation to ask if they knew anything about him. None of them did, so after the St Andrew's Day service, he approached Jack directly. Jack told him his story, and when the Rector found that he had a good knowledge of the Bible and Prayer Book, he asked him if he was prepared to go to the northern part of the State each Sunday to take services. After some hesitation, Jack agreed, and throughout the winter made a long journey by sleigh to take services in lumber camps.[2]

He also started studying Latin and Greek, and before long life was so full that he resigned from his job on the railroad. When summer came, he was given another responsibility. There was a St Paul's School as well as a St Paul's Church in Concord, attended by the sons of well-to-do parents. The school ran a summer camp for boys from less well-to-do families in Boston and New York, and Jack was asked to take charge of this, which he did.

The next two years were happy ones for Jack, only marred when he had a fall while mountain climbing with the boys from the camp, necessitating an operation and a period of going slow. He decided to undertake some theological training and obtained a scholarship to a Divinity School in Connecticut, but on one occasion, when he visited the lumber camps, he was accompanied by a bishop, who suggested it would be wiser to go to Selwyn College, Cambridge, from which his brothers had graduated. (In those days, a Theology degree at Oxford or Cambridge was sufficient qualification to enter the Church of England ministry, without the need to attend a Theological College.) To go to Cambridge involved finding the necessary fees, but Jack had recently received a legacy, so he sent a telegram to Selwyn, was accepted without needing to take any entrance examination, and nine days after sending the telegram, having crossed the Atlantic

---

[2] Ibid.

Vocation and Ordination 1907–1913

on a White Star liner, he found himself an undergraduate.[3]

Jack was of course a good deal older than almost all the other students, but mixed with them easily and naturally. Having lived for years in surroundings that were not exactly academic, he found he had to work hard, but he found time in the long holidays to return to Concord for the summer camps.[4] He usually crossed the Atlantic on the *Lusitania* and got to know several members of her crew. It would be a great sadness for him when the liner was sunk by a German submarine in 1915, with the loss of 1,200 lives.

During Jack's last year at Selwyn, he was approached by a number of people offering posts for him after ordination. The one that appealed to him most, not surprisingly, was one that would again involve going overseas. The approach was made by C F Andrews, who later became famous for his friendship with Mahatma Gandhi, for his contribution towards the Gandhi-Smuts agreement, and for publishing a book in which he described how he had adopted the lifestyle of the poorest of the poor in the subcontinent. Andrews was at this time working for the Cambridge Mission to Delhi, and he was looking for someone who would undertake special work among English-speaking people in the bazaars. In due course, Jack accepted the invitation, was made deacon by the Bishop of Ely in Great St Mary's, Cambridge, and sailed for India with, as he remarked, 'a very different outlook on life, a marked contrast to that when I went to Ceylon.'[5]

---

[3] Ibid.
[4] Weller, C H, *A Few Notes Concerning the Edward Wellers*.
[5] Weller, J R, *Bishop over the Andes*.

The Middle East and Marriage 1913–20

When he arrived in Delhi, the first thing Jack discovered was that the local committee of the Cambridge Mission did not agree with C F Andrews that the work for which he had recruited Jack was the Mission's responsibility. The bishop was away in England, so Jack was asked if, until the bishop's return, he would teach Hindus and Muslims and run their sports at the Mission School. He did this, and at the same time prepared for the exam he would have to pass before being ordained as a priest. He also began to learn Urdu.

When the bishop returned, he sent Jack north to Lahore, to be Assistant to the Chaplain at St Andrew's Church, which served Anglo-Indian workers in the railway workshops. He was ordained to the priesthood there, in Lahore Cathedral. He enjoyed the work, and he and the Chaplain related well together and achieved the building of a daughter church at Moghulpura, where the railway authorities were building houses for their employees. Jack was allocated one of the houses, and was thus in a position to contemplate marriage.

While he was at Selwyn, Jack had made the acquaintance of an undergraduate at Girton College named Alexina Caley. Since then they had kept up an infrequent correspondence, and in the meantime Alexina had achieved a double first in Modern Languages and had remained at Girton as a lecturer. Jack now wrote inviting her to come out to marry him, asking her to respond by cable, and to his delight she replied that she would come. The story goes that, having not seen her for some time, Jack was not at all sure that he would recognise Alexina when she stepped off the boat, but he managed to do so, and they were married in Bombay (now Mumbai) Cathedral, with just the priest, verger and one friend present as well as themselves.

Before he left Lahore, Jack had been informed that, as a wedding present, the railway company would provide him with the

The Middle East and Marriage 1913–20

use for two weeks of a carriage, which they could attach to any train they liked, enabling them to visit any places of interest they wished without needing to book into hotels, as the carriage was equipped for sleeping. Particularly memorable were their visits to the Taj Mahal, which they saw in daytime and by moonlight – 'a sight one can never forget' – and to Gwalior, where the Maharajah was celebrating his birthday, and provided them with an elephant for sightseeing and a guide who took them to places not usually accessible to European visitors.

When they finally got back to Jack's bungalow, which he had furnished in the hope of making it suitable to receive a lady, he found that a woman's ideas were very different from his, but had to acknowledge that the result of the changes she made was infinitely more attractive and comfortable than what he had prepared. They had the fun of unwrapping their wedding presents and settling down to life in their home, but this was not to be for long.[1]

The First World War had now broken out. Jack, having missed the action in South Africa at the end of the Boer War, volunteered for combatant service, but was told that the only function he could perform was that of Chaplain. He was sent first to Waziristan, north of Lahore, where he had his first experience of frontier warfare. Then he was ordered to go to Beled, north of Baghdad on the Tigris, to join the 2nd Dorsets, a battalion that was part of the 3rd Lahore Division.

He was there for many months, which were rather dreary, waiting for an enemy attack. As padre he organised the mess and various sports. He even played a game of rugger for the last time; it took him many days to recover. Eventually the battalion was ordered to move forward by forced marches to take part in an offensive, which was successful, and then they were withdrawn and ordered to go to Palestine via Egypt.

They were encamped near Ismailia in Egypt for some time, which gave him an opportunity to visit Cairo and the pyramids. He won a race with some of the other officers to reach the top of the Great Pyramid; his time was twenty minutes. However, while in Cairo he had a severe recurrence of malaria, which had

---

[1] Weller, J R, *Bishop over the Andes*.

The Middle East and Marriage 1913–20

troubled him for some years, and was taken by stretcher to hospital. Soon after he returned to his unit, they completed their move to Palestine, camping near Lod.

Jack was now Divisional Chaplain, and the division's general gave him an opportunity to visit Jerusalem, which General Allenby had recently captured. Jack had the privilege of celebrating Communion at St George's Cathedral. Soon afterwards, his division formed part of Allenby's army, which advanced to Damascus. Another attack of malaria was accompanied this time by dysentery, and he was sent back to hospital in Egypt. Then a message came from India to say that Alexina was very ill and not expected to live.

Jack was given permission to return to India, and he had great difficulty in finding out where Alexina was, and even whether she was still alive. He eventually tracked her down to Simla, in the foothills of the Himalayas north of Delhi, and he found that she was indeed very ill, though over the worst. He also found that she was as worried about him as he had been about her, as this was the time of the influenza epidemic which carried off so many people in that year.[2]

The bishop now arranged for Jack to go to Karachi and assist the chaplain there, who was overwhelmed by the number of troops passing through on their way back to England for demobilisation. Jack and Alexina lived in a hotel there for six months, during which Alexina made an excellent recovery from her illness. Then came a posting to Quetta, where there was a house for them, so they had the pleasure of unpacking all their treasures and having a home of their own again. However, once again, this did not last long, as war flared up in Afghanistan and Jack was ordered to join the 4th Quetta Division. He spent most of 1919 at Chaman on the Afghanistan border, but was back in Quetta in the early hours of Christmas morning, able to undertake a full programme of services on that day.

Life now became a constant round of lunch parties and dinner parties, which Jack and Alex found very boring and not the kind of work Jack had entered the ministry to do. So they decided to sacrifice his pension and incur the financial loss involved in his

---

[2] Ibid.

resigning from his work so that they could return to England. No boats from India were available for some time, so they travelled to Ceylon, where Jack saw many old friends whom he had known in his tea-planting days. They obtained berths on a cargo ship and thus returned to England.[3]

---

[3] Ibid.

Missions to Seamen 1920–34

Jack now had his first taste of work in an English parish. He and Alexina went first to Dordon in Warwickshire, where Jack's brother Chris was the parish priest. Chris was on a visit to the United States, and Jack deputised for him until his return. Then he accepted the post of curate of Christ Church, Greenwich, a dockland parish on the south bank of the Thames in London. The parish was understaffed, so the work was very arduous, but it involved contact with all sorts of people, and Jack and Alexina much enjoyed it. One abiding memory was that there was so much unemployment in the area that the dockworkers did not dare to take time off on weekdays even to get married. The result was that many weddings had to be squeezed in between services on Sundays. Furthermore, standards of literacy were such that getting couples and their witnesses to sign in the right spaces in the marriage register was a difficult and time-consuming task. Jack and Alexina were not able at first to find suitable accommodation in the area, but eventually they were able to purchase a small house, which meant that once again they had all their belongings around them.

However, yet again it was not to last. The Missions to Seamen (now named The Mission to Seafarers) maintains bases in ports all over the world where seafarers, far from home, can be welcomed and provided with food, refreshment and entertainment. The organisation approached Jack, asking if he would take charge of their work in Buenos Aires. He refused, but not long afterwards they approached him again, this time producing strong arguments for why he should go to Melbourne, Australia on their behalf. Australia was one part of the world with which Jack was not familiar, and, after much thought and prayer, he and Alexina decided that it would be right to accept this invitation.

The outward journey was not a pleasant one. There were 1,200 emigrants on board, so the boat was crowded, with little privacy, and 'worst of all, and most wearing, was the everlasting jazz music from morning till night'. Jack wrote a strong letter of protest to P&O, but Alexina would not let him send it. The redeeming feature of the seven-week journey was the celebration of Christmas on the day after they left Cape Town. Jack was Father Christmas, giving presents to the children – 'never shall I forget the cheers of joy which went up from that crowd of youngsters! I have had some thrilling Christmas parties in different parts of the world, but this transcended them all.'[1]

The Mission had three Institutes in Melbourne, and Jack's predecessor had organised things well, so he needed to make few changes. The exception was that there was a 'chucker out' whose task it was to eject anyone who became obstreperous after drinking too much. His presence was resented by the clientele, so Jack undertook the task himself; this meant that 'for some time my life was pretty hectic and full of incidents which drew upon all my tact and physical strength', but after a time he gained a reputation for toughness and they were able to carry on without the bouncer.

There was a local Ladies' Guild of 1,500 members who were responsible for providing entertainment at all three Institutes, running canteens, cinemas, concerts, plays, card parties and dances, and arranging picnics and trips into the country. The hours of work for the chaplain were long, but it brought Jack into contact with all sorts and conditions of men.[2] As he put it, 'much that was sordid had to be grappled with, but on the whole it provided a grand opportunity of making friends with a fine lot of fellows.'[3]

Jack managed to get a month's holiday each year, which gave him and Alexina a chance to explore the country. Particularly memorable was their last holiday, when they walked up the east coast of Tasmania. They came to like the Australian people very much, and were sorry when their time in that country came to an end after five fulfilling years.

---

[1] Weller, J R, *Bishop over the Andes*.
[2] Kingsford, M R, *The Mersey Mission to Seamen 1856–1956*, Abbey Press, 1956, p.83.
[3] Weller, J R, op. cit.

Unexpectedly, a cable arrived asking Jack to take up a post at the headquarters of the Mission in London. This represented a promotion, but what really influenced Jack to accept the invitation was the fact that both his mother and Alexina's were growing old, and they felt that after an absence of five years they should be nearer to them. The journey home was a luxurious one, in contrast to the outward one, after they had been given a 'send-off such as only Australians can give.'[4]

The post to which Jack had been appointed was that of temporary General Superintendent of the Mission, deputising for the Superintendent himself, who was on sick leave. He was responsible for interviewing and appointing applicants for chaplaincies all over the world, as well as fulfilling preaching and speaking engagements around England, visiting Mission Stations at home and on the Continent, and, of course, office work in London. This was not the kind of work for which he felt fitted or which he enjoyed, so when the year was completed, in spite of the possibility of his being appointed Superintendent on a substantive basis, Jack instead applied once more to be placed in charge of one of the actual Missions.

One important Mission where the post of Chaplain-Superintendent had just become vacant was on Merseyside. The Revd Lord Thurlow had held the post for the previous eight years,[5] for the last four of which he had also been Rural Dean of Liverpool, but he had now resigned at the age of seventy. Jack decided to apply for the post.

When he went for his interview in Liverpool, Jack was shown the Mission's Central Institute and was horrified by its unattractive and old-fashioned appearance and drab decorations, making it much inferior to Institutes he had seen overseas, and totally inappropriate for the present generation of seamen. He met the chairman of the committee which would be interviewing him, who asked his opinion. 'It needs a bomb' was his reply. 'You are the man we want,' said the Chairman.[6]

Another problem was that the Chaplain's house was in Sefton

---

[4] Ibid.
[5] Kingsford, *The Mersey Mission*, op. cit., p.146.
[6] Weller, J R, *Bishop over the Andes*.

Park, some way from the Institutes where his work lay. Jack resolved to solve both problems by raising funds for a complete refurbishment of the Central Institute, which would include the provision of the Chaplain's flat on the top floor. The building had also for some years included sleeping accommodation for twenty-five to thirty-five people, but this was no longer needed, as the Gordon Smith Institute and the Sailors' Home catered for the needs of those requiring overnight accommodation,[7] and Jack had ideas for the better use of the space. Opposition had to be overcome, but the necessary funds were raised and the refurbishing project successfully carried out – a process that included rewiring and much reconditioning. It took twelve months to complete.

A feature of the Institute when it reopened in 1932 was a 'Club for Junior Officers and Apprentices', situated on the second floor and consisting of a self-contained suite of rooms, including a billiard room and a writing room as well as a canteen and lounge. The Mission's historian records that this was 'a great and permanent success', and indeed it urgently needed enlargement three years later.[8]

These were days of high unemployment, and Jack was struck by the number of elderly seamen lounging about on the streets, with inadequate pensions and little or no prospect of any further employment. He set aside a room in the refurbished Central Institute to be called the 'Ancient Mariners Club', expecting about one hundred people to show interest. In fact many hundreds did so, and a constant stream of 'Ancient Mariners' took advantage of the facilities.[9]

Amongst the seamen who visited one or other of the nine institutes for which Jack was responsible were on many occasions ones whom he had previously encountered in Melbourne. One of his gifts was a remarkable memory for names and faces, and men were often surprised to find themselves addressed by name.

When Jack had a break of a few days, he and Alexina drove up to the Lake District, where the Treasurer of the Mission had a

---

[7] Kingsford, *The Mersey Mission*, p.83.
[8] Ibid, pp.83–84.
[9] Ibid, p.84.

house by Lake Windermere, which he made available to them on a number of occasions. They loved the scenery and the contrast it provided with their urban existence. Jack's time at the Mersey Mission was comparatively short, but very fruitful. It ended in 1934, when major changes took place in his life.

Bereavement and Consecration 1934

The great sadness of Jack's life occurred when his much-loved wife died of cancer after a long illness. Alexina had given him wonderful support throughout the years of their marriage, and his diaries in subsequent years, when his travels took him to interesting and beautiful places, often contained comments like 'Alexina would have loved this'.[1]

In the months that followed his bereavement, Jack received much kindness and sympathy, and a considerable number of offers of new posts from people who felt he would be glad of a change of scene. These included parishes in England, and Mission to Seamen posts in other parts of the world. Jack replied to all of them by saying that so far he had made no plans.

Then, very unexpectedly, he received a letter from the Archbishop of Canterbury, Cosmo Lang, inviting him to stay a night at Lambeth Palace. He wondered what this might mean, and he was 'astounded' when the Archbishop asked him if he would accept the post of Bishop of the Falkland Islands – a diocese which at that time included all Anglican work in South America to the west of the Andes, from Panama to Tierra del Fuego, as well as the Falkland Islands themselves, and South Georgia. The cathedral was at Port Stanley in the Falkland Islands, which were the only part of the diocese that was British territory.

Jack's answer was that he did not feel he had the necessary qualifications, to which the Archbishop replied 'that is my business.' Jack left Lambeth with a promise that he would think and pray about the offer and give a response as soon as possible.

For the next week, Jack considered all the implications of the Archbishop's invitation. One factor that influenced him was that Alexina, when she was dying, had said, 'God has some piece of

---

[1] Diary entry 1/10/34

work for you in which I am not required.' At the end of the week, Jack informed the Archbishop that he accepted the offer.[2]

The Consecration took place at Southwark Cathedral on St Peter's Day, 29 June 1934. Archbishop Lang presided; the Archdeacon of Liverpool preached. The hymns included 'Our Blest Redeemer', which invoked the Holy Spirit – something Jack once told the present writer he did every day. Other hymns included 'Through the Night of Doubt and Sorrow' and 'For All the Saints', both perhaps chosen with the memory of Alexina in mind.[3]

After the service, Jack gave a lunch for the twenty-four members of the family who were present. These included his brother Morton, who came over from Scotia, New York, for the occasion with two of his daughters. A photograph was taken after the meal, reproduced below.

Three months later, Jack set out for his new diocese.

Family party for lunch after the Consecration. Jack in the centre is flanked by the other two Johns present – Dr John Churchill, aged ninety, who was the other bridegroom when Jack's parents were married in Chesham sixty-two years earlier, and the present writer, Jack's nephew and godson, then aged nine. Jack's three clerical brothers, Chris, Morton and Dick, are behind him.

---

[2] Weller, J R, *Bishop over the Andes*.
[3] Southwark Cathedral – Order of Ceremonial of the Consecration.

Journey to the Falklands I 1934

Travel in the 1930s was much more leisurely than it later became. Jack went by sea. As he set out, he wrote in his diary how he thought about 'the new life absolutely different from the old for which I seem so inadequate, yet I believe it to be in response to no uncertain call of God.'[1] The ship called at various ports in France and Spain. In the latter country he visited Santiago de Compostela, and of course it brought him into contact with the Spanish language, with which he would need to be familiar in his diocese. They then visited Bermuda and some of the West Indian islands. Some of his fellow passengers were returning to the West Coast of South America; 'they seem anxious to meet me and they tell me that I am right up against things, some of them in a way which sounds as though they are proud of the fact.'[2]

The ship reached the Panama Canal on 18 October, and Jack was shown the machinery chambers and control room at Gatun Lock; he was much impressed when the 22,000 ton vessel was raised eighty-three feet in one and a quarter hours. Two days later, they at last reached Jack's diocese, after three and a half weeks of travel, docking at La Libertad in Ecuador and discharging passengers. The next day they reached Paita in the extreme north of Peru, and a member of Jack's staff, Archdeacon Foley Whaling, came aboard. Jack commented, 'He looks a man and is certainly doing a man's job'.[3] They had a two-hour talk, and Jack gave him his blessing and said he hoped to visit him again in the following year.

Two days later the boat reached Callao, the port for Lima, the capital. Jack was met by the British Consul and the Chaplain and was transported in style to the Legation, where a magnificent lunch for twenty was provided. A car was put at his disposal, and

---

[1] Diary of J R Weller 27/9/34
[2] Ibid 29/9/34
[3] Ibid 21/9/34

the Chaplain and the Missions to Seamen Lay Reader showed him the church and told him about their work. 'They both have a very difficult task. The Church and its work is ignored except on ceremonial occasions such as Armistice Day when everyone turns up. I was introduced to a handful of regular attendants.'[4]

Paita and Callao were two of a number of small British communities scattered down the west coast of the continent. Some of them were a thousand miles apart, but, even so, there was a good deal of coming and going between them, and naturally there was a good deal of discussion, inside and outside church circles, about the new bishop and what he was like. He was told it was reported that he was *simpatico*. It was also reported that he was partial to lemon pie. This was a result of appreciation he had expressed when one of his first hostesses gave it to him for lunch. As a consequence, everywhere he went as he continued his journey down the coast, he was fed with the same sweet course.

Six days after leaving Callao, the ship reached Valparaíso, the main port of Chile. It was also the headquarters of the diocese, as it was roughly in the centre, allowing the bishop to travel north or south to visit the various chaplaincies. Until the Panama Canal was opened, it had also been possible to reach the Falkland Islands fairly easily from there, as there was a frequent service of ships of the Pacific Steam Navigation Company going through the Straits of Magellan, and it was traditional for the bishop to be granted free passage on them. Now that the Canal provided easier passage between the Atlantic and the Pacific, very few ships made that voyage, and the usual alternative was for the bishop to go by train to Buenos Aires, to cross to Montevideo, and to catch a small vessel to the Falklands from there. The journey cost £40, which, Jack remarked, was 'a record price for a Bishop in any part of the globe to pay for transport from his residence to his Cathedral.'[5]

Once again, Jack was met off the ship by the local chaplain, whose name in this case was Gunstone, and by the Lay Reader in charge of the Missions to Seamen Institute, Buchanan. Once his luggage was cleared through customs, he sent it on to the Institute, where it would stay until he decided where he would

---
[4] Ibid 23/10/34.
[5] Weller, J R, *Bishop over the Andes*.

make his base. He was then taken to lunch at the house occupied by his predecessor, where Gunstone was now living, but he quickly decided that it was too large and expensive for him to run. In the afternoon he was shown one of the two Anglican churches in the city, St Paul's, and the Missions to Seamen Institute, both of which were well cared for. He spent the night in the suburban home of the British Consul, where he would be staying for the duration of his visit to Valparaíso. Two days later, he obtained his *Carnet* (Identification Papers) on which the Chilean authorities insisted, and was intrigued that the process involved the taking of no less than six copies of his fingerprints. The same evening he was shown the other of the two churches: St Peter's.

The next day was All Saints' Day, and Jack took his first service in his new diocese at St Peter's: a Communion Service for a congregation of forty-five. In the afternoon he had a very welcome chance to relax, as he had the Consul's house and garden to himself. He was very struck by the glorious profusion of flowers in the garden, and commented that 'the smell, the atmosphere, the sun and the shapely gum trees make me very homesick for Australia.'[6]

He met many church members again on the following day at a reception. 'The people are a curious mixture, some English born and Scotch born, some the result of English and Scotch marriage with Chileans (Spanish and Indian). They will need very careful handling, as I know from experience that crossbreeds are always ready to believe that they are being slighted because they are not thoroughbreds.'[7]

The following Sunday was a busy one. He preached at St Paul's in the morning and St Peter's in the evening, and on both occasions 'quite a good congregation came to have a peep at me'. In between there was an official luncheon, when some leading people were invited to meet him. Meals were becoming something of a problem for him. 'I shall have to be careful or I shall be killed by kindness. The meals I have to attend seem endless. They are good trenchermen out here.' Slabs of meat were served even before the five courses. 'I really must make some rule about food

---

[6] Diary of J R Weller, 1/11/34.
[7] Ibid, 2/11/34.

Journey to the Falklands I 1934

that will not offend my hosts. The trouble is they are touchy people and will say "Our food is not good enough for the bishop" if I refuse to eat it.'[8]

A few days later, Jack went in a very comfortable train to Santiago, the capital, and a chauffeur-driven car took him to the Embassy, where he was to stay with Sir Robert and Lady Michell. Jack's eldest sister, Mollie, was married to a Keith Michell, who was a relative of Sir Robert. Another connection was that the Ambassador had served as a trooper in South Africa at the end of the Boer War at the same time as Jack. So, although Jack had been received in a somewhat formal fashion when he first arrived, the atmosphere soon thawed.

The second day after Jack's arrival in Santiago was Armistice Day. The Anglican church was a small one, and it was packed for the 10.30 service and again for a children's service in the afternoon. Jack returned to Valparaíso the following day, after the Michells had invited him to stay again at the Embassy whenever he was in the capital.

On his previous visit to Valparaíso, Jack had booked two rooms in a dwelling on a hill near St Paul's church, which would be his base for the time being. On his return, he stayed for a few nights in a hotel while the rooms were being made ready, and took services in both churches on the Sunday. A few days later he was able to move his possessions into the rooms, much to his relief, and then he set out once again for Santiago, this time on his way to visit, for the first of many times, one of the Missions that were at work among the indigenous people. When he arrived at Santiago, 'I was met by two Churchwardens and a Council Secretary, a queer trio. The Secretary was rather full of liquid. The whole organisation of the Church here needs cleaning out badly.'[9]

---

[8] Ibid, 5/11/34.
[9] Ibid, 23//11/34.

Journey to the Falklands II 1934–5

Jack spent the next three weeks being introduced to the work among the indigenous people. The Mapuche (then known as the Araucanians) had never been conquered either by the Incas or by the Spaniards. However, when Chile broke free from Spain and fought successful wars with Peru and Bolivia, it turned its strong and well-equipped army against the Araucanians in the late 1880s. A treaty was signed which had the effect of incorporating the tribe as part of Chile, but it led to looting, disease, starvation and a drastic reduction in numbers.

The South American Missionary Society had begun work among the Araucanians soon after they were incorporated into Chile. It had been hard going, for the only 'doctors' to whom they went were witchdoctors, and there was a great deal of drunkenness. Jack commented, 'All Araucanians ride from early childhood, and are excellent horsemen. Many hundreds of them, in fact, seem to have nothing else to do for the greater part of the year than ride from one drinking booth to another, and then leave it to their horses to take them home.'[1] However, the policy of establishing boarding schools at various points was now bearing fruit, and Jack was given enthusiastic welcomes at every centre he visited.

On the day he arrived, Jack travelled by train through country that reminded him of the Yorkshire moors He was met at Temuco, the headquarters of the Mission, by Canon Wilson, in charge of the work, and by five of his colleagues. After lunch at the Canon's house, Jack was travelling again, being driven for seventy-five miles over very bad roads, crossing two rivers, and reaching Tolten at 7 p.m., to be greeted by the ringing of the church bell and a road lined with 120 Mapuche schoolchildren waving flags, who gave him cheer upon cheer. He inspected the buildings, which had been put up recently by the local

---

[1] Weller, J R, *Bishop over the Andes*.

missionary, Miss Yates, at her own expense. There were schools for boys and for girls, including boarding accommodation, a surgery and dispensary, and a large modern church.

The next day was Sunday. Jack celebrated Communion at 8 a.m. in English, with just the Mission staff present. At 10 a.m., there was matins in Spanish, and Jack was fascinated by the appearance of the congregation – the men wearing their best brightly-coloured ponchos in his honour, and the women, who had Mongol-type faces, also wearing their best clothes, adorned with the silver ornaments which had been handed down from generation to generation and had escaped the looting which had occurred after the incorporation into Chile. Jack gave an address through an interpreter, and pronounced the blessing in Spanish.

Then, after just enough time for a meal and a pipe, there was a long service in Mapuche. It included songs which members of each hamlet had practised for Jack's benefit, and an address by a young Mapuche. Jack again gave the blessing in Spanish, and there was just time for the evening meal before he conducted a Confirmation for eight women and twelve men. This was rather a strain, as it involved a good deal of reading in Spanish, but instead of preaching he gave his notes to Canon Wilson, who based a sermon upon them in Spanish. The service ended at 10.15, bringing a very busy day to an end.[2]

Jack's hectic first few hours in the Mission area set the tone for the rest of his three-week stay. There were long journeys over very bad roads – on one occasion a car in which he was being driven broke an axle and on another a tyre flew off and the driver went happily on for some way before it occurred to him to change the wheel. One road was judged to be unsuitable for cars at all, so he had to go by horseback. It was the first time in sixteen years he had ridden a horse, and he was understandably stiff afterwards.[3] He took several Confirmation services; 'My Spanish seems to be understood when I am reading it.'[4] Everywhere there were enthusiastic welcomes, performances of one kind or another, and services in one or another of three languages. One of the stations he visited was

---

[2] Diary of J R Weller, 25/11/34.
[3] Ibid, 29/11/34.
[4] Ibid, 02/12/34

staffed just by one lady, a Miss Brooke, who ran a day school for local children and held services in people's homes. She had been there for five years and lived surrounded by cats, dogs, parrots, a pig and a hare, but she was ten miles from the nearest white person.[5]

A fortnight after his arrival, Jack took the chair at a meeting in Temuco of representatives of all the stations in the Mission area. There were 'several knotty problems', but 'all went well', and Jack was congratulated on pushing the business through so that they finished after a mere three hours.[6] Jack summed up his stay in the area by writing that he was impressed by the work of the missionaries – 'they all seem to be doing a splendid work.'[7]

On his way back to Valparaíso, Jack called at Concepción, which is further south, on the coast. 'The church is the nicest I have yet seen and the people are all very friendly and hospitable. There is only a small English community here...the problem of keeping a padre here is great; first not enough money, second not enough work, and yet these splendid people ought to be served.'[8]

Jack decided on this occasion not to travel across country to Buenos Aires, but to try to get a passage through the Straits of Magellan by ship. So he continued his journey southward, but got held up at Magellanes, owing to a strike of wharf labourers. This gave him an opportunity to visit some of the *estancias* (ranches) in the extreme south of the continent. Again the distances were vast. He travelled 700 miles, and visited one farm with 250,000 sheep on 500,000 acres. He was told of another, which he would be invited to visit on a future occasion. It was nearly as big as Yorkshire, one of a group which covered 65,000 square miles – the size of Ireland.

On 23 January, Jack managed to get a passage on the *Clan Macquarrie* – a ship which had often called at Melbourne when he was working there. As he boarded her, he was greeted with the words, 'Hullo, hullo, what are you doing in this part of the world?' by one of the crew members.[9] The ship took him to Port Stanley, and he thus completed the final stage of his initial journey, four months after leaving Liverpool.

---

[5] Ibid, 11/12/34.
[6] Ibid, 07/12/34.
[7] Ibid, 03/12/34.
[8] Ibid, 11/12/34.
[9] Weller, J R, *Bishop over the Andes*.

South Georgia, Argentina and the North 1935–6

Throughout February and March, Jack was responsible for the parish of Port Stanley, as the dean was on leave. He lived alone in the Deanery, but found life somewhat frustrating; 'There has been nothing for me to do, a few sick people to visit and a few services to take'.[1] He could not leave the town as there were no roads, and even excursions on foot were difficult, as the ground was boggy and it was usually blowing a gale.

At the beginning of April, there came a chance to break the monotony. A ship was going to South Georgia, and he was offered the opportunity to visit the southernmost part of his diocese. No bishop had ever been there before, though a former dean had visited the island some years previously.

The 800 mile journey was a stormy one – 'I lost two of my meals as soon as I acquired them' – but he was rewarded when they arrived in brilliant sunshine. The sea was bright blue and he was able to admire a magnificent spectacle of 'hills and ... snow-covered mountains with here and there a glacier running right down to the sea.'

One morning he took a Communion Service for ten people in the magistrate's drawing room – 'no one remembered when there was a previous service.'[2] Another highlight of his visit was a trip out to a huge whaling factory ship, the Norwegian *Sven Foyn*. The only way to get on to the 22,500-ton ship was by going up a rope ladder which was covered in whale grease; 'the stench was anything but pleasant'. He was shown all over the ship and given an excellent lunch; the Norwegian food made a welcome change from the everlasting mutton he usually lived on in those parts. He described the visit to the ship as 'one of the most interesting days I have had.'[3]

---

[1] Diary of J R Weller, 04/35.
[2] Ibid.
[3] Ibid.

South Georgia, Argentina and the North 1935–6

The same evening, Jack was given another excellent meal by the manager of the shore factory, who also presented him with two whales' teeth and a whale's eye, the latter of which had been dried in formalin. There were said to be only fifty of these in existence, and Jack showed his to very many people, all of whom said they had never seen anything like it before.[4]

The return trip to Stanley was also a rough one; for two days after he got ashore, the rooms appeared to be moving about. On his return, he stayed with a doctor and his wife in a delightful house. While he was there, a cable arrived from Chile, asking if he could find someone to take services in Santiago, as the Chaplain was seriously ill. His comment was 'Not a hope – soon I shall be the only man in the diocese.'[5]

During Holy Week and Easter, Jack conducted services in the cathedral and was rewarded with a good response from parishioners. One old lady said, 'I have never known such congregations, dear Bishop, you know it is your face that does it.'[6] He urged them to continue to attend services in good numbers, but sadly, he doubted if the progress made would continue after the return of the dean, who was not popular.

While he was at Port Stanley, an incident occurred which showed Jack's remarkable memory for names and faces. A man called Tom Oates called to present him with an invitation to dinner. 'Is your name Oates by any chance?' Jack asked. 'Didn't I meet you in Melbourne in 1921? You were an apprentice in the square-rigger *William Mitchell*?' Actually the person he had met was the man's brother, but as Tom Oates remarked, 'My goodness what a memory.'[7]

It was clearly important to get back to the South American mainland, so, soon after Easter, Jack went by ship to Montevideo in Uruguay. His plan was then to cross the River Plate to Buenos Aires; from there to fly to Gallegos, in the extreme south of Argentina, and then to cross over to Magellanes, in the south of Chile, where he was due to conduct a Confirmation. However,

---

[4] Weller, J R, *Bishop over the Andes*.
[5] Diary, 04/35.
[6] Diary, 25/04/35.
[7] Letter from Tom Oates, 08/03/37.

this involved obtaining a visa for entry into Argentina, and, since the people of that nation felt as strongly as they did fifty years later about their claim to the 'Malvinas', an application from someone styled 'the Bishop of the Falkland Islands' was not regarded with very much favour. First there was a refusal, then a demand for $80, which Jack eventually managed to get reduced to $20.

Even with the visa, Jack was at first refused entry when he arrived at Buenos Aires, and had visions of being charged another $20, or even of being held to ransom; however, after 'considerable unpleasantness', he was eventually allowed in. On the day after his arrival, he called on the bishop of Argentina and Eastern South America, whom he described as 'a most lovable man'. It transpired that the bishop knew more about events in the Falklands diocese than Jack himself did. He told Jack that the lay reader who was looking after the churches in Valparaíso and Santiago had died three weeks previously. So Jack had to change his plan, and he booked a passage on a 'Transandine' train to Valparaíso. Before his departure, he took part in a Jubilee Service at the cathedral, which was attended by the President of the Argentine and many senior officials. Jack was amused by the fact that the President, seated at the front of the congregation, had to look at the bishop of the Falkland Islands.[8]

After a spectacular journey through the Andes, Jack reached Valparaíso in the middle of the night, and was met by three men who had booked rooms for him and who brought his letters – 200 of them. He commented in his diary, 'What a wonderful life it is!'

For the next three months, Jack remained in Valparaíso, dealing with administration, and taking services at the church in Santiago as well as at the two in Valparaíso itself. Towards the end of the year, a chaplain arrived to look after the three churches, leaving Jack free to visit the northern part of his diocese. He was able to keep the promise he had made in the previous year, and see the work that Archdeacon Whaling was doing in northern Peru and Ecuador. This was satisfactory, as was the work of the Revd S A Davies in Lima, but it was farther south that he found serious problems. There was an area which included Arequipa in southern Peru, in the foothills of the Andes; Antofagasta and

---

[8] Weller, J R, *Bishop over the Andes*.

Iquique, which are ports in northern Chile, and La Paz, the capital of Bolivia, which is across the Andes. All these towns had previously had their own chaplains, but dwindling numbers of church members meant that a single priest had to undertake the almost impossible job of caring for these small and widely-scattered congregations. Jack experienced for himself what the task involved, visiting each of the congregations. The previous chaplain's health had broken down, but a new one was due to arrive, and Jack comments 'we trust he will be able to stand up to the hardship of continued travelling from sea level to great heights and back again.'[9]

---

[9] Letter from J R Weller to Canon J McCloud Campbell, 29/09/36.

'The Flying Bishop' 1936

Early in 1936, Jack was able to make his postponed visit to the extreme south of the continent to conduct confirmation services, but it was already clear to him that a very high priority was recruiting clergy for his understaffed diocese. This was underlined when a cable arrived, saying that the chaplain in the Falkland Isles had been forced to leave after only five months, because his wife's health had broken down as a result of the harsh climate and conditions of life. The only way to find the clergy he needed was to return to the UK. He could not afford the time to make two more crossings of the Atlantic by sea, so he asked Mrs Lilford Price, whom he described as 'a very capable person who acted as a kind of "universal aunt" to English and American people in Valparaíso' to make the necessary bookings to enable him to cross the ocean by air.[1]

It was a long journey, starting at the Chilean port of Punta Arenas, on the Magellan Straits. He left there at 4.30 one morning in a mail car with two other passengers, bound for Rio Gallegos, on the Argentine coast, 185 miles away. The road was a rough one, and on arrival it was found that one of Jack's suitcases had fallen out of the canvas on the carrier of the car. The driver obligingly retraced his journey for two hours during the night, and was able to retrieve the suitcase.

Meanwhile, Jack was provided with overnight accommodation by a young English couple (he knew the wife's parents), and the husband, who was a small man, lent him a pair of bright red and blue pyjamas, which were 'never meant for my figure'. Jack wondered if he would be able to extricate himself in the morning, but managed to do so, and, reunited with his suitcase, boarded the plane for Bahia Blanca, south of Buenos Aires. On the train to the capital, he found that Bishop Every, the Bishop of Argentina, was

---

[1] Weller, J R, *Bishop over the Andes*.

a fellow traveller, so they took the opportunity to discuss many matters of mutual concern.

On arrival at Buenos Aires, Jack learnt that Mrs Price had arranged for him to proceed by seaplane to Rio de Janeiro, where he would board a German airship, the *Graf Zeppelin*. Having been roused at 2.30 the next morning, he boarded the seaplane, which flew low up the coast, rewarding him with spectacular views, not least when it circled Rio harbour two or three times before splashing down. He was entertained by members of the local church, and learnt that the airship on which he would be travelling was not the *Graf Zeppelin*, but the *Hindenburg*, which had only entered service in the previous month and was on her first trip to Rio.

The *Hindenburg* had been designed to be lifted by helium, but American regulations required hydrogen to be used instead. The danger of this was tragically demonstrated in the following year, when the airship was destroyed by fire with the loss of thirty-six lives. That, however, was in the future. On the morning of his departure, Jack was roused at 2.45 and conveyed by special train to the mooring place of the airship, which was in a large hangar. The accommodation was quite luxurious, with a cabin for each passenger. As the *Hindenburg* became airborne, the motion felt like that of a ship on a very smooth sea, with a swishing noise as it passed through the air. Communication was possible by radio-telephone, and there was a foretaste of what was to come when, at dinner on the second night out from Rio, Jack received a phone call from a reporter, asking if he was enjoying his trip. This resulted in a headline the next day: 'The flying Bishop says his bed is comfortable'.[2] As the *Hindenburg* passed Recife, Jack found time to send one of the airship's special postcards to the present writer; it is one of the latter's most treasured possessions.

As the airship approached Gibraltar, a bolt of a connecting rod of one its four engines broke, which meant a 15% loss of speed, a problem that was compounded by strong headwinds. This did not affect the passengers, but it involved a change of route, as it would no longer be possible to fly across the Bay of Biscay and up the Channel to Germany. Also, for a time, radio communication

---

[2] Ibid.

failed, leading to grave concern that there had been a disaster, but this was a false alarm. The German authorities asked permission from the French for the airship to cross their country, and this was reluctantly given on condition that it did not deviate more than 10 km from the River Rhone; numerous French aircraft escorted it in and made sure the ruling was observed.

The airship reached Friedrichshaven after four and a half days in the air. When it arrived, journalists sought out the most interesting passengers for their stories, and, not surprisingly, the English ones were soon writing about Jack. He told them that he was pleased to complete the journey so quickly and that accommodation on the Hindenburg was as good as that on a liner, so he had enjoyed every minute of the flight.[3]

One journalist wrote, 'The first person to descend the gangway after the huge airship was moored was the fair-haired, blue-eyed, ruddy-faced smiling Bishop'. This led some of his nephews to dub him 'the ruddy Bishop',[4] but the title 'The Flying Bishop' was the one that the press used in their subsequent reports.

The flight to Croydon (which in those days was a major commercial airport) from Friedrichshaven required a stop at Stuttgart, and, as it happened, Adolf Hitler was at the airport at the same time and passed within a few feet of Jack. The Channel was crossed in a snowstorm, and more journalists were waiting when the plane touched down. Jack told them about his work, and *The People* carried the headline 'Farm labourer becomes "my Lord Bishop"' and went on to provide a sympathetic summary of what he had done in the last two years:

> Not only does his diocese demand that he be a flying Bishop, but a sailor, horseman, motorist and mountain climber as well. A journey of 1,500 miles by air is mere routine for him [...] Fifty miles in the saddle to some lonely settlement is just taken in his working stride. Motoring on the swamp-like roads, ditched for hours, then pulled out by oxen – is just what he had learned to expect. The Bishop smiled reminiscently. 'I get plenty of travelling on my job. On a tour of the northern part of my diocese, which lasted four months, I was rarely more than a day in any

---

[3] *Daily Express*, 13/04/36.
[4] Weller, J R, *Bishop over the Andes*.

one settlement, and five days was my longest halt. It is impossible to provide a chaplain on small settlements of sixty to seventy people, and in some of the places I visited they had not had an English Church service for over seven years.'[5]

In spite of all the favourable publicity he received, Jack's search for 'six athletic chaplains for unoccupied stations in my diocese – healthy young fellows fit enough to stand the rough life out there' was only partially successful. At this time, the Cunard liner the *Queen Mary* had just been completed and was about to make her maiden voyage to New York. Jack was offered the post of Chaplain, which would have got him across the Atlantic in four days, but he had not yet recruited the clergy he was seeking, so he had to decline. Eventually, having found three of the six men he needed, he decided to return to his diocese via the USA and Canada, hoping to find the others in a part of the world where people were more used to roughing it. So he booked a passage on the Queen Mary for the ship's second Atlantic crossing. Shortly before the ship was due to sail, Jack received a letter from Cunard offering him a magnificent suite for the crossing, and he thus began his journey home.

---

[5] *The People*, 19/04/36.

Extra Responsibility and Breakdown 1936–8

Jack acted as Chaplain on the Atlantic crossing, celebrating Communion on the Sunday for a congregation that included a Japanese Admiral, his wife and his daughter. On arrival in New York, Jack found that American reporters were even more of a trial than their English counterparts. They wanted to photograph him together with a well-known film star who had also made the crossing. 'I don't know her,' Jack said, but that was easily remedied and the introductions made. 'I may sound very ungallant,' Jack told her, 'but I do not wish to be photographed with you.' So the photos were taken separately – but in the evening papers they appeared side-by-side under the caption 'Passengers who arrived on the Q.M. today'. As Jack remarked, it is difficult to discourage the American reporter.[1]

Jack's brother Morton was a priest in the United States, and the brothers now set off on a 5,000-mile tour of much of the USA and Canada, lasting four weeks. Jack had spent so much of the last two years travelling and would have been glad to have had a rest, but on the other hand he needed to interview some Canadian clergymen who had expressed interest in serving in the Falklands or South America, and he also had many long-standing friends, people he had known long before during his many years in North America, with whom he was glad to renew acquaintance. He was successful in finding the recruits he needed for his diocese, being particularly pleased to have found a young Canadian and his wife who had 'both been accustomed to rigorous weather and working among isolated people' and who would, he had every hope, be able to withstand the climate and living conditions, and to minister successfully in the Falkland Islands.

In August Jack returned to Valparaíso by ship, having been away for just over five months. In the following month he wrote a

---

[1] Weller, J R, *Bishop over the Andes*.

report for the Archbishop of Canterbury. He stated that his visit to England was 'on the whole satisfactory'. It had produced many applications to work in the diocese, but the majority of those applying were quite unsuitable. They had not yet been ordained, whereas he needed men with some experience of parish work. However, he had found a young chaplain for Valparaíso, and an older, experienced man for northern Chile, as well as the Canadian Chaplain for the Falklands. He commented, 'this leaves the diocese with one vacancy – Magellanes – which is a great improvement on this time last year when there were five vacancies.'[2]

Jack learned that the Araucanian Mission had been passing through a difficult period, since communist agents had been at work, and one of the boys' schools had needed to be shut down for some weeks. He had visited the Mission on his first arrival in the diocese, and he now did so again. The following extract from his account of the visit gives a clear idea of what was involved.

> After two days' travel, I arrived at the headquarters of the Mission late one afternoon, and was asked to give almost immediate answers on innumerable questions. The following morning early I started for Tolten. The roads being better than last year, we were able to make the journey of sixty miles in just over five hours. I visited schools etc. and preached at Evening Service. Early next morning I set out for Llican, a missionary outpost. The road was very bad, and I had considerable difficulty in approaching and leaving ferries on account of the mud ... The next morning I took a celebration in English for the staff. The morning service was in Mapudungu, but I gave the address in Spanish, which I had to read, and I conducted a Confirmation in the evening. The following morning a Communion Service in Spanish, after which Canon Wilson and I rode on horseback to Negue, a place about nine miles distant, for the day. The next morning we left Tolten for Maquehue, where we started the same kind of programme over again.[3]

During this visit, an important step forward was taken in the development of the Mission: the first move towards an

---

[2] Letter from J R Weller to Canon J McCloud Campbell 29/09/36.
[3] Weller, J R, *Bishop over the Andes.*

indigenous ministry. A meeting was held, attended by at least 500 people. The women and children formed a circle around Jack and the missionaries, while the men, 150 or 200 of them, sat on their horses outside the circle, according to custom. The people were informed that if they wanted their own priest, they would have to raise the necessary money, and a good number came forward and promised that they would contribute.

There was one outstanding candidate, and although his name – Antinao – was not mentioned, it was probably clear to everyone that he was the person Jack had in mind. Jack wrote of him, 'He stands out a long way ahead of the others [...] He knows the Saviour, and to my mind is sufficiently equipped for the work of preaching to the primitive minds of the Mapuches.' Jack hoped that the enthusiasm for raising the money would not wane when the time came to collect it (something the Mapuches themselves would do), and he expected to make Antinao a deacon on his next visit.[4]

Early in 1937, Jack received a letter from the Archbishop of Canterbury, asking if he would assume responsibility for Anglican work in the whole of South America by succeeding Bishop Every, who had been Bishop of Argentina and the eastern part of the continent, including Brazil, for the last thirty-five years. This would restore the situation of some years previously; transport difficulties had made it necessary to divide the work on the continent into two dioceses, but with greatly improved communications by air it was felt this division was no longer necessary.

Jack accepted the invitation, and in a letter to Canterbury he set out the advantages of treating the work on the continent as a unity. 'This sounds a tremendous task, but in reality it is not as great as it sounds.' As events were to prove, this assessment was rather optimistic. Jack added, 'The distances are tremendous, but there is a perfectly splendid airway system in South America, and moreover two points of the Falkland Islands Diocese, that is to say Magellanes, and the Falkland Islands themselves, are much more easily reached from Buenos Aires than from Valparaíso.' He added that if the continual travelling proved to be more than could reasonably be demanded of one man, the obvious solution was to provide him with a suffragan. So, in April, 1937, Jack

---

[4] The *SAMS Magazine* February 1937 pp.15–16.

moved his headquarters from Valparaíso to Buenos Aires.[5]

Many in Chile were sorry to see that Jack would no longer have his headquarters among them. An 'English Colleger' from Temuco wrote to the *South Pacific Mail* stating that

> ...Chile has had a wise and generous spiritual leader in its midst while it had Bishop Weller [...] Wherever one goes in Chile, one sees, or hears, evidence of what Bishop Weller has done. It may be connected with the well-water or other simple needs of a little mission-station; or it may even concern the maintenance of an English School for girls in a place like Temuco [...] The Araucanian can be as conscious of receiving the most kindly consideration at the hands of Bishop Weller as the British Ambassador or any other, whether in a high or low place in life [...] He is a patient listener, a kindly speaker and a shrewd observer. The magnitude of his new undertaking does not appear to daunt Bishop Weller. Somehow, he manages to take everything in his stride – with signs of enjoyment rather than of strain.'[6]

A few days after his move, Jack provided the Missionary Council of the Church Assembly in England with some statistics that had been requested, giving a picture of his diocese as it was before the amalgamation: 'The figures for the British population in this diocese show that the communities are steadily dwindling. The whole total of population (British) being 8,880, of which 2,400 live in the Falkland Islands, leaving a total of 6,480 scattered up and down the west coast so that fifty per cent of this total of 6,480 would be a fair estimate of the number of Anglicans on the West Coast, not including Araucanians.' He added that most of the congregations were financially self-supporting, the exceptions being the problem area of Antofagasta, and, to a lesser extent, Santiago and Valparaíso.[7]

Jack was enthroned in Buenos Aires, at a service which caused the local newspaper to inform its readers that 'seldom, if ever, can a more impressive and colourful ceremony have taken place in St John's Pro-Cathedral.' Included in a capacity congregation were representatives of ten other churches, including two Orthodox

---

[5] Weller, J R, Bishop over the Andes.
[6] The *South Pacific Mail*, 13 May 1937.
[7] Letter from J R Weller to Canon J McCloud Campbell 04/05/37.

clergy in their colourful robes. The Commission appointing the bishop was read out and must have sounded rather intimidating, being addressed 'to all Christian people to whom these presents shall come and more particularly to the clergy and laity of the Church of England in Argentina and in Eastern South America, Uruguay, Paraguay, Bolivia and Brazil'. This of course only referred to Jack's new diocese, geographically the largest Anglican one in the world. He was still responsible for his former diocese of the Falkland Islands, geographically the second largest.

Jack now set out on a programme of visiting congregations for whom he had undertaken responsibility in Argentina and Brazil, and this involved 'a great variety of travel in the cold climate of the South, in the heat of Brazil, on the pampas and in the heights of the Andes'. Not surprisingly, he felt in need of a rest, and when he returned to the west coast for weekend visits to Santiago and Valparaíso, he retired to spend the intervening days in an obscure hotel in the heights of the Andes. However, soon after his arrival he was taken seriously ill, and, after a long and painful journey back to Valparaíso, he was admitted to hospital suffering from a complete breakdown and gallstones.[8]

After three months, he was allowed to return to England, arriving on the *Orbita* on 4 April 1938. He was still far from well and was ordered to rest for several months. He commented, 'Throughout my life I have at all times been beset with the feeling that I must be up and doing, with the result that over and over again I simply asked for a breakdown. During my married life, my far-sighted wife used to apply the brake; now there was none to cry halt! when the pace became too swift.'[9]

The South American Missionary Society made no demands on him in this time, although he was able to attend a meeting of their General Committee in May. He reported that the Archbishop of Canterbury had approved the plan for the appointment of an assistant bishop, but this did not happen immediately, as the first two names of possible candidates sent to the Archbishop were not accepted.[10]

---

[8] Weller, J R, *Bishop over the Andes*.
[9] Ibid.
[10] Minutes of the General Committee of the SAMS, July 1938.

Frances Butler, Jack's second wife

Marriage and Return to the Diocese 1938

During his time at the Mersey Mission, Jack had become very friendly with the Mission's treasurer, Mr Percy Kipling, and his wife. It was they who used to make a house by Lake Windermere they owned available to Jack and Alexina when they needed a holiday. Mrs Kipling had a companion called Frances Butler, and now in 1938, as Jack recovered from his breakdown and pondered the reasons for it, he began to consider the possibility of marrying again, and his thoughts turned to Miss Butler. She was almost thirty years Jack's junior and was very hesitant when he first proposed to her, but eventually she agreed to marry him.[1]

The press for a time had much to say about the forthcoming marriage and the difference in age between the partners, but to Jack's relief the Dean of Canterbury entered into a marriage where the age difference was even greater, and this distracted the journalists' attention. He and Frances were married quietly in London.

Towards the end of the year, Jack had recovered sufficiently to be able to return to his diocese. Visits to the chaplaincies in Brazil were a priority, and, in view of the climate, he and Frances thought it would be best for him to make the journey alone, reserving her first taste of South America for the time when she could join him in Buenos Aires.

One of the first places Jack visited was Para (now Belém) at the mouth of the Amazon. 'The climate, to say the least, was trying. Perspiration streamed off me throughout my visit.' The chaplain there, Miles Moss, had been there for over twenty-five years, without receiving a salary. He was very capable, a fine musician, a keen entomologist – and rather eccentric. He had a reputation for interrupting his sermons if he saw a rare moth fluttering about one of the lights at the evening service. He would

---

[1] Weller, J R, *Bishop over the Andes*.

Marriage and Return to the Diocese 1938

grab a net, capture the specimen, and then resume his sermon. 'He did great service to the church, and was much loved by everybody.'[2]

In most places, receptions were planned in order for people to meet Jack, and in Para there were two of these: one for English expatriates, the other for indigenous people. At the latter, speeches tended to be rather lengthy, and it was after midnight before Jack got to bed. He was called at 4.30 the next morning, in order to catch his plane, and even after this early start he reached his next port of call only just in time to get a quick bath before attending a reception. 'This kind of thing was physically exhausting, because it happened so frequently. Nevertheless, I enjoyed the experience.'

By contrast with Para, another of the chaplaincies that Jack visited on his way through Brazil was one where the climate was delightful. This was the gold mine at Morro Velho, about 250 miles from Rio de Janeiro. There was a British community there of about 300, mostly from County Durham on four-year contracts. The chaplain and his wife ran the church and also the school, and were paid for by the mining company.

While he was there, Jack was shown a block of gold, valued at £5,500 and weighing about 56 lbs. He was told that if he could lift it up and carry it away with one hand, it would become his property. What his hosts did not realise was that his life as a labourer before he was ordained had left him with powerful muscles, and he succeeded in lifting the block, but unfortunately not in carrying it away. He was not given a second opportunity![3]

Soon after Jack's return to Buenos Aires, Frances joined him. There were more British people in that city than in any other in South America; a large majority of the 45,000 Britons who lived in Argentina lived in the capital. During the few weeks before they set out on their travels together, Frances was welcomed at a large number of receptions, lunch and dinner parties, as well as many church services.

One problem that Jack faced was that of paying for his own continual travelling. He had been warned on his original ap-

---

[2] Ibid.
[3] Ibid.

pointment that his predecessors (who were all men of independent means) had paid their own travelling expenses and that he would be expected to do the same. He realised that, in fairness not just to himself but to his successors, this was an unsatisfactory situation, and he succeeded in getting most of the centres to accept responsibility for paying for his travel when he visited them. All the centres, apart from the Missions, were, of course, unlike English parishes, self-supporting; there were no endowments.[4]

---

[4] Ibid.

An Ordination and an Earthquake in Chile 1938–9

One of the first trips that Jack and Frances made together was to visit the isolated *estancias* in the south of Chile and Argentina. The drives were long, and Jack remarked, 'Frances had many new experiences. Accustomed to first-class cars on English roads, never had she experienced so much mud and dust, or the frequent negotiation of streams, with the water splashing above the running-boards. There was one stretch when we ran into real dust, and on arrival at the *estancia*, our host and hostess could not refrain from bursting into laughter.'[1]

Once again, Jack's phenomenal memory for people came in very useful, as he often found links with his hosts; one came originally from Melbourne, so they had many friends in common because of Jack's time with the Missions to Seamen in the Australian city.

The Christmas of 1938 was spent with a large Welsh community at Esquel in southern Argentina. Attendance at the Communion Service was disappointing, as most of the people were chapel folk, but another service later in the day was well attended. Jack wondered when the next Communion would be held there, as the nearest chaplain was 600 miles away.[2]

The next part of the journey was a very spectacular one, as it involved travelling through Chile's Lake District. They crossed several lakes by launch 'with snow-capped mountains towering above us'. They had intended to stay for a few days at a place called Peulla, where the scenery was particularly magnificent, but because of a very unpleasant fly called the *coliwacho*, which attacked them and bit Frances' legs badly as soon as they went out of doors, they decided to continue their journey. This gave Jack an opportunity to introduce Frances to the spectacular view of the

---

[1] Weller, J R, *Bishop over the Andes*.
[2] Ibid.

volcano Osorno, before they booked into an hotel at Puerto Varas on the coast.

Jack's plan was now to pay another visit to the Araucanian mission stations. They went first to one of them, Cholchol, where an event of great importance took place. Juan Antinao had served faithfully as a deacon and was now ready to become the first Araucanian priest. Another man, Segundo Cayul, had been prepared to be made deacon. So, on 23 January, Jack had the joy of performing the ordination service.

Araucanian ordinations, 23 January 1939. Juan Antinao, the new priest, is on the bishop's right; Segundo Cayul, the new deacon, is on his left.

He wrote, 'This was no hasty action, it had been looked forward to and prepared for almost from when the Mission was started forty years ago … this in some ways must mark the end of the old regime; from now on gradually the Native Mapuche Church will be staffed and guided by men of its own race – that is the ideal behind it all, a Mapuche Church for the Mapuche race.'[3] On the same afternoon, Jack held a Confirmation for twenty candidates, and he ended his description of this memorable day with the

---

[3] The *SAMS Magazine*, May 1939, p.54.

An Ordination and an Earthquake in Chile 1938–9

words, 'This glorious vision of a Native church is only just visible; there is a long journey in front of us yet before we stand aside.'[4]

Jack and Frances went on to visit other stations, ending with Cautinche, where Antinao was in charge and where Jack conducted another Confirmation. Then, since they were tired, they retired to bed early on their return to Cholchol.

They had not long been asleep when they were woken by the first tremors of a major earthquake. Although they were some distance from the epicentre, a good deal of damage was done, with several small buildings destroyed, and water tanks and chimneys brought down. Jack had invited several of the local clergy to meet him for a conference, and while those who had been long in the country were unperturbed, one or two of the newcomers found it a terrifying experience.[5]

The earthquake killed 28,000 people. When news of it reached Buenos Aires, the Archdeacon, who only knew that Jack and Frances were 'somewhere in Chile', was very concerned and sent cables to various places where he thought they might be. Eventually his mind was put at rest by a report from the British Ambassador in Santiago.

Jack's intention had been to visit next the British community in Concepción, further up the coast, but he had to abandon the idea as it was impossible to get through. Instead, he and Frances boarded the first train to attempt the journey to Santiago. It had to crawl over some very bad spots, but eventually it reached the capital, where they stayed at the British Embassy.

The return journey was made via Mendoza, on the Argentine side of the Andes, then by air eastwards for 250 miles to Cordoba. There was no service there, as there were few British people and the church was only used occasionally, but the objective of the visit was Los Cocos, a spectacular car's journey up into the hills. There the church ran the Allen Gardiner Memorial Homes, where British children who had lost one or both parents were housed and educated. Jack commented, 'They have splendid buildings in beautiful surroundings. Mrs Miles, who has been in

---

[4] Ibid, p. 55.
[5] Weller, J R, *Bishop over the Andes*.

charge for eleven years, has done splendid work in turning out some boys and girls equipped to take their place in the world – a chance they would not otherwise have had.'[6]

The twenty-four hours that Jack and Frances spent at Los Cocos concluded with a reception, which ended at 6 p.m. Five minutes later they were on their way by car back to Cordoba, where they caught the overnight train to Buenos Aires. The whole trip had lasted just under three months, during which, apart from a stay in Santiago which included two Sundays, they had never been in one place for more than four or five days.

Understandably, Jack and Frances were keen to have accommodation of their own, and, a couple of days after their return to Buenos Aires, they moved into a small flat, beautifully furnished, situated near diocesan headquarters and very central for everything else.

Jack's stay in the capital lasted only a week, after which he left Frances to get things moved into the flat while he boarded a plane to Trelew, on the coast about 500 miles to the south. This was the centre of another community of Welsh origin, and in his four days in the district, Jack's programme included three Communion services, one Confirmation for nine candidates, two other services with sermons, two receptions at which he had to make speeches, and three talks in the school, as well as taking part in a long conference about school and church matters.[7] Then it was back to Buenos Aires in time for Holy Week and Easter, after which, apart from a forthcoming visit to Northern Argentina, he hoped to have six months occupying the flat, administering the diocese and preparing for Synod.

---

[6] Memo by J R Weller – copy in author's possession.
[7] Ibid.

Chaco Mission and Synod 1939

On the Thursday after Easter, Jack and Frances were off on their travels again. They had visited congregations and missions in the south and west of the continent, and the time had now come for them to travel to northern Argentina, where the South American Missionary Society had been at work for fifty years. It began with a train journey of 1,000 miles to Embarcación, where they were met by one of the missionaries, the Revd B A Tompkins, who drove them in a Ford truck to the nearest centre of the Mission. The people among whom the missionaries were working, the Chaco, were very different from the Araucanians of Chile – much more primitive and not nearly so robust. They had practically no possessions and for generations had been nomadic, though now that Mission centres had been established with a church, school and dispensary, they tended to settle near them and regard them as 'home'. They made Jack and Frances very welcome, seeking to shake hands with them even when they had gone to bed.[1]

Jack always liked to say at least part of the Confirmation service in the candidates' own language, so he went into the forest and practised over and over again saying the words 'Defend O Lord this thy servant' in the local Matako tongue. This was much appreciated, in spite of the fact that, after he had confirmed a large number of people, he began to run the words together so that he was now saying 'Defend O Lord this man's hat.'[2]

Jack was extremely impressed by the dedication of the missionaries. He wrote that theirs was

> ...an exceedingly arduous task, carried on at a great distance from civilisation. Living conditions are particularly difficult, and for a portion of the year, the climate is, to say the least, trying. Yet among those engaged in this work are some who have been there

---

[1] Weller, J R, *Bishop over the Andes*.
[2] Ibid.

Chaco Mission and Synod 1939

> twenty-five years or more, with only occasional leave. The matter of food is always a problem, as the land is not very fertile. The main food of the missionaries is pumpkin and goat, supplemented by canned foods, the latter used very sparingly, as transportation is very difficult and expensive. The water supply, at times inadequate, has a variety of flavours, some, as I know from experience, not altogether palatable.[3]

He added, after describing how he had been bitten by a poisonous spider, with consequences from which it took him two months of treatment and diet to recover, that

> It is only right for the reader to apprehend something of the conditions under which the work of the church is being carried out [...] We were fully prepared to put up with the discomforts for a few weeks, but my wife and I fully agree that we would not care to undertake what these men and women are doing, and have been doing, some of them for many years [...] A man needs have a very special call.[4]

Another of the problems in this mission district was the difficulty of travelling from one centre to another, because of the state of the roads. They discovered this a couple of days after their arrival in the area, when they made what should have been a two-hour journey between two of the Mission Stations. Frances was driving and they came to the top of a steep hill when Tompkins shouted, 'I forgot to tell you – the brakes are not functioning!' The truck careered around trees and mud holes, and ended up stuck in a deep water patch. It had been anticipated that there might be a problem at this point, so a buggy drawn by mules had been sent there to assist if needed. Jack took the controls of this for the next three miles, and eventually the truck, which had been freed after seven hours' hard work, caught up with them and took them to their destination after a journey of twelve hours, not two – and without food. Further journeys also required assistance from the mules, and there were times when they passed through water which came up to the animals' bellies.[5]

---

[3] Ibid.
[4] Ibid.
[5] Ibid.

Chaco Mission and Synod 1939

A few days later, they had another eventful journey between Mission Stations. The truck got stuck in mud at nightfall, so there was no alternative to sleeping where they were. They found a comparatively dry spot, and after a meal of sardines and biscuits, which was all the food they had, they settled down for the night. During the night, Jack felt something soft and slimy touching the bald patch on his head, which was right up against the mosquito net. Thinking it was a snake, and keeping as still as possible, he asked Frances to shine a torch. It revealed a bewildered frog, which was catching the mosquitoes that had been attracted by the bald patch.

In the morning the truck resisted all efforts to extricate it from the mud, so Jack, Frances and Tompkins, after a breakfast consisting of more sardines and biscuits, set out to walk to their destination, which was still fifteen miles away; but fortunately, after three miles, they were met by a sulky (a two-wheeled buggy) whose driver had been sent to look for them. Later there was another tiring journey through mud and water to the nearest railway station, and Jack commented that it was one 'which might have thrilled us had we taken it a few weeks earlier. However, we had had sufficient of that kind of thing to satisfy our yearning for adventure.'[6]

The journey back to Buenos Aires involved passing through Paraguay. They stayed in a hotel in Asunción, the capital, but were informed that it would not be possible to visit the local missions, as the roads were impassable. Jack did so on a number of later occasions, and found that they were very different again from those in either Chile or the Argentine, being based on *estancias* with large herds of cattle, which solved the food problem.

Now Jack could at last look forward to a stay in Buenos Aires, where he could occupy the flat, catch up with administration and prepare for Synod. It was normally the custom to hold a Synod for the Diocese of Argentina every three years, but for various reasons one had not been held since 1934. It was now possible to hold one, but not easy, owing to the distances involved; usually only those clergy who lived within 1,500 miles of the Argentine capital were able to attend.

---

[6] Ibid.

Chaco Mission and Synod 1939

There had been a delay about the appointment of a Suffragan Bishop, because Archbishop Lang, who had always maintained a close interest in Jack's work, had turned down both the names of possible candidates submitted to him in the previous year.[7] However, he had now accepted that of the Revd J Evans, and, in a message sent before Synod, he asked Jack to 'assure your Synod, when it meets, of my deep and constant interest in the welfare of your vast diocese. I trust that the advent of Bishop Evans will strengthen and extend the Episcopal oversight of the diocese and relieve you of a heavy burden.'[8]

The outbreak of the Second World War inevitably cast a shadow over the Synod's proceedings, and in his charge to the diocese, Jack affirmed

> 'Christianity has something to say to a world faced with a crisis of unparalleled magnitude: that there is that in Christianity which can provide the remedy [...] No greater calamity can befall the Church or the individual than to lose sight of the ideal of holiness.'

He added,

> 'The Christian sees in the present trial something more than the [...] simple conflict between confronting armies. He perceives in it the struggle against principalities, against powers, against the rulers of the darkness of this world, against spiritual evil in high places. It is a struggle between good and evil.'[9]

---

[7] Minutes of the General Committee of SAMS July 1938
[8] Buenos Aires press report.
[9] Ibid.

Journey to Panama I 1939–1940

Every ten years, the Archbishop of Canterbury summons all Anglican bishops to a Conference at Lambeth, and the next one was due in 1940. Jack decided to take six months in visiting first the south of his diocese and then the various congregations up the west coast of the continent before setting off for England from Panama: 'a trip which provided us with the greatest variety in the shortest time.'

The first stage of the journey took Jack and Frances back to the Welsh colony at Trelew, on the Atlantic coast approximately 500 miles south of Buenos Aires. They arranged to continue their journey southwards in a hired car, but the owner refused to go because of the appalling condition of the roads. The only alternative was an old seventeen-seater bus, complete with driver, and for the next fifteen days they travelled approximately 1,500 miles through Patagonia sitting on very hard seats in what became known as the 'Episcopal Coach'. On a number of occasions they had to get out and help the driver dig the bus out of the mud in which it was stuck. They stopped at several *estancias*, where Jack conducted services and in some cases baptisms. The country was very flat and they travelled 'mile after mile without seeing a rise of ground worth calling a hill.'[1]

There was rather an embarrassing situation one evening, when they booked into an hotel and the proprietor made an objection. In this isolated part of the Roman Catholic country, he was unaware that it was possible to be a married clergyman. Passports were produced and he allowed them to stay, but they felt he was not really convinced that it was all above-board.[2]

Their route followed the coast for many miles, giving them a view of hundreds of seals basking in the sun. They also saw a few

---

[1] Weller, J R, *Bishop over the Andes*.
[2] Ibid.

herds of guanaco and quite a number of rhea, the South American ostrich. At one *estancia* where they stayed the night, there was a gathering of members of a large family, many of whom had come a long distance; it was the first visit of a clergyman for a very long time, and there were a number of baptisms to perform.

As they continued their journey southwards, they at last came to rising ground and to snow, which made a welcome contrast to the heat they had experienced at the time they left Buenos Aires. Eventually they booked into the Cosmos Hotel in Punta Arenas, said to be the southernmost hotel in the world.

Jack hoped to be able to visit the Falkland Islands while they were in the south of the continent, and he enquired of a naval officer whether a ship would shortly be travelling to the Islands; it was a privilege of the bishop to have the assistance of the Royal Navy when required. The answer was that a cruiser would shortly be available to take him, but it would not be returning to the continent. Jack decided not to take the risk of being stranded on the islands. A few days later he heard that the cruiser in question, HMS *Achilles*, was one of the three ships which ended the career of the German pocket battleship the *Graf Spee*, in the Battle of the River Plate, and Jack and Frances wondered whether they had just missed being involved in that historic encounter.

Jack and Frances now began the long journey northwards up the west coast of the continent. Their ship encountered what Jack described as 'the worst gale I have encountered in many trips' in the Gulf of Pena, but the spectacular scenery was some consolation. They stayed in 'a horrible little hotel' at Puerto Monte before continuing their northward journey to Valparaíso, then Santiago; a journey that they accomplished a good deal more easily than in the previous year, in the immediate aftermath of the earthquake.

At a height of 14,500 feet, on the border between Chile and the Argentine, there is a large and impressive statue of Christ, his hand raised in blessing. Beneath is the inscription '*May the rocks of these mountains crumble into dust before the peace between Chile and Argentina is broken*'. While they were in Santiago, Jack, Frances and two companions hired a car with a very skilled driver to take them up to see the statue. After a spectacular but hair-raising journey they reached it in an area which was 'barren, desolate, but truly magnificent'.

Jack made his way to a quiet spot a little apart from the road and opened his Prayer Book, for the Revd J Evans was due to be consecrated as a bishop in Westminster Abbey. Jack had sent him a cable assuring him of the prayers of his future colleague. Now, while they were up by the statue, was the actual hour of the Consecration, so Jack read some of the prayers from the Consecration Service and felt that 'far away, amid the awe-inspiring peaks, we played our vicarious part in the Consecration.' He later heard that his cable was actually handed to Bishop Evans as he was entering the Abbey for the service.[3]

---

[3] Ibid.

Journey to Panama II 1940

By now, war was raging in Europe, and it affected Jack and Frances on the next stage of their journey. They embarked on the SS *Orduna*, and found that it was 'blacked out' at night, and took rather a circuitous route to their destination. This was Antofagasta, which was the residence of the chaplain who was responsible for a part of Jack's diocese which had always caused him a great deal of concern. This was because it consisted of a number of British communities scattered over a vast area, including La Paz, the capital of Bolivia, which was hundreds of miles to the north, high up in the Andes.

Antofagasta had once been a thriving port, with a large number of residents engaged in the nitrate business, but the British community now numbered only 200. Jack's task was to visit their church and those of the other communities, conducting Confirmations, meeting church committees, and attending receptions which had been arranged 'to meet the bishop'. The next stop was Iquique, about 100 miles up the coast, and here, too, the British community was much reduced, numbering about 120. However, Jack found it to be a very happy community, and, thanks to two outstanding laymen, services had been held every Sunday, whether or not the chaplain was available. Iquique was also the first place, as they travelled northwards, where it was pleasant to swim; farther south, the Humboldt current made the water too cold for enjoyment.

The journey next took them inland, up into the Andes. Jack knew from experience that it would be best to gain height gradually, giving him a chance to get acclimatised, so after a hair-raising journey of 250 miles by car to Arica, where they visited the four British residents, they went by plane to Arequipa in Peru, which is 8,000 feet above sea level. Jack took the first service that had been held there since his last visit, four years previously, and he and Frances were taken on a drive through the neighbouring countryside, where they saw a number of llama convoys.

For the next stage of their journey to La Paz, they were given the use of a railway coach which had two bedrooms, a living room with a dining table, a kitchen and a lavatory, and they lived in it in comfort for six days. The railway was climbing all the time, at one point reaching 14,700 feet, and Jack was full of admiration for the engineering skills of those who had constructed it. After three days at Cuzco, where there are Inca ruins, they boarded a miniature liner which took them across Lake Titicaca. The ships on this lake had been made in England, shipped in sections to the coast and then transported to the lake, which is at an altitude of 13,000 feet, where they were reassembled.

The British community at La Paz numbered about 120, mostly employed on the railways. Jack took a Confirmation and Communion service in the Legation, and a service for a much larger congregation in the Canadian Baptist Mission Church later in the morning. He was given the loan of a car in which he made a 150 mile journey through the surrounding countryside, surrounded by towering mountains, enabling them to see herds of llamas and alpacas – and they also saw many mirages.

On their journey back to the coast they stopped at Oruru, a railway place where fifty people attended a service in the evening, followed by a reception and a dinner party. The next morning, Jack celebrated Communion, after which they boarded a train for the twenty-four hour journey back to Antofagasta.

After a couple more days in the port, during which Jack conducted two Confirmation services in the outlying area, he and Frances continued their journey by sea, landing at Callao, the port for Lima, the Peruvian capital. There, too, the chaplain was responsible for ministering to copper and silver mining communities up in the mountains, but in this case it meant ascending to even greater heights, and the chaplain for much of Jack's time was liable to mountain sickness, so the communicants had to come to him rather than the other way round. On one of his visits, Jack did indeed go up into the mountains to minister, and it left him feeling very glad he did not have to live at 15,000 feet.[1]

The next stage of the journey was by air to the oilfields in the extreme north of Peru. Once there had been a chaplain there who

---

[1] Weller, J R, *Bishop over the Andes*.

also ministered to people employed in other oilfields over the border in Ecuador, but for years now the community had been served by occasional visits by the chaplain from Lima, 700 miles away. However, local laymen had made a delightful little chapel in the Club House where services were held and had also established a Sunday School. Jack had a busy three days there, as there had been no visit from a chaplain for a very long time and there were many children to be baptised.

Jack's next task was to visit the communities in Colombia. He had seen records of one or two visits by chaplains to these communities, but none of one by a bishop, and he wanted to see if more satisfactory arrangements could be made for the Anglicans in that country. He visited Bogotá, the capital; Medellin, where he took Maundy Thursday services for a 'small but enthusiastic' congregation, and Cali, where he conducted a well-attended Good Friday service. On the train back to Buena Ventura on the coast, they met a bank manager and his wife who had been in Colombia for fourteen years without seeing an Anglican priest. So, at 5 a.m. on Easter morning, in the bedroom of the hotel where they were staying, Jack celebrated Communion for them and Frances. They then took the boat for the last stage of their journey to Panama.

There, he called on Bishop Beal of the American Episcopal Church and came to an agreement with him about ministering to the Anglicans in Colombia. As Jack remarked, 'Any point in Colombia could be quite easily reached by plane in a very short time by one of his chaplains in the Panama zone, whereas our nearest chaplain was 2,000 miles away.'[2]

Jack and Frances had now completed a journey which had taken them exactly six months. They calculated that they had packed fifty-nine times and attended sixty-six receptions. Frances had opened dozens of garden parties and sales of work, given away prizes at schools throughout the diocese and spoken at many women's meetings. Jack commented, 'I know she enjoyed every moment of our travels together, whether they were in luxury and comfort or in the mire and mud of the Chaco; the fact that we were together was all that mattered.'[3]

---

[2] Ibid.
[3] Ibid.

Fatherhood and Synod 1940–42

The journey to Panama had been intended to be followed by an Atlantic crossing to attend the Lambeth conference of bishops, but in the meantime World War II was raging, and the Conference was postponed. Jack and Frances were much in need of a rest after their long journey, so they went by ship to New York, where they were able to obtain the lease of a summer house in the White Mountains. It was comfortable and well-equipped, and was remote enough to give them the solitude they required. This was a part of New Hampshire that Jack had known well during his years in the USA, and they did a good deal of hiking over tracks he had last travelled thirty years previously.

Jack had written to Archbishop Lang, saying he would like to make a contribution to the war effort, perhaps by driving an ambulance, and he asked the Archbishop to signify by telegram whether he agreed to this – 'come' if the answer was 'yes', 'proceed' if the answer was 'no'. One day, as Jack and Frances were basking in the sun outside the house, a large car drew up and two enormous federal policemen alighted. They demanded to see Jack's papers and the maps he had been using. They then wanted to know the significance of a cable he had received consisting of the word 'proceed', and they also wanted to know why he had been receiving letters from all over South America. It took Jack some time to persuade them that he was a bishop, not a German agent; apparently some German agents had been rounded up in a neighbouring state, and the policemen had thought they might be about to make another capture. Jack commented, 'it made me realise the Americans were right on the job in that anxious 1940.'[1]

Towards the end of the year, Jack and Frances returned to Buenos Aires by sea, visiting the Brazil communities on the way. On their return they held a reception in St John's Hall, where

---

[1] Weller, J R, *Bishop over the Andes*.

many friends came to welcome them back after their long absence.[2] Much of the administration of the diocese in their absence had been carried out by Canon Townsend, 'a most efficient secretary' without whom, Jack wrote, 'I simply could not have coped.'[3] Even so, there were many matters requiring decisions from Jack, so he spent a good deal of time in Buenos Aires after his return, going off from time to time to conduct Confirmations.

In 1941, there occurred an event which meant that, for the time being, Frances could no longer accompany Jack on his travels. As an (erased) entry in the minutes of the S. American Missionary Society's General Committee put it, 'an important and happy domestic event was expected to take place in the Bishop's household', and it duly did with the birth in Buenos Aires of their daughter Elisabeth on 1 August.

For the time being, Bishop Evans took responsibility for many of the visits to chaplaincies and Missions which Jack would otherwise have done, but there was no shortage of matters requiring Jack's attention in Buenos Aires. The Argentine government passed legislation affecting foreign property owners, requiring that the authorities should see books relating to cash, lists of members, minutes of meetings, and inventories. The SAMS Committee in London felt that a lay missionary would be the person most suited to the requirements of the work in the north of the country, and Jack agreed, provided the spiritual work of the Mission remained under the guidance and control of the clergy.[4]

At this time there were forty clergymen at work in the two dioceses for which Jack was responsible. Six were Missions to Seamen chaplains, eight worked among the indigenous people, three were engaged in educational work, and the remaining twenty-three were ministering to British expatriate communities. Between them, in 1941, Jack and Bishop Evans conducted forty-three Confirmation services, in places ranging from Belém in the

---

[2] Report in local press.
[3] Weller, J R, *Bishop over the Andes*.
[4] Minutes 14/01/42.

Fatherhood and Synod 1940–42

far north of Brazil to Santa Cruz in the far south of Argentina.[5]

In 1942, another Synod of the Diocese of Argentina was due to take place, and it duly convened in October of that year, with delegates coming from all the countries in which the diocese was at work, and one to whom Jack gave a special welcome as a representative of his other diocese, the Falklands. Since the last meeting, Archbishop Lang of Canterbury had retired, but he wrote to Jack, assuring him that although 'I have no longer, alas, any official connection with your vast diocese, I shall always take the deepest interest in its welfare and your work.'[6] Lang's successor, William Temple, also sent his greetings. 'The diocese must be unique', he wrote, 'in the difficulty which it suffers through the vast distances which separate one part of it from another, making especially hard the building up of that sense of family life around the Bishop as Father-in-God, which is the joy of diocesan work ... but I know in how great a degree this difficulty has in fact been overcome through the leadership of the bishops.'[7]

In his Charge Jack said, 'There has been much during the last three years for which to thank God in the life and work in the diocese.' He specially mentioned 'the steady progress made in the Spanish-speaking work under the guidance of the chaplains of St Saviour's, Belgrano', the success of the Ordination Candidates Fund, the value of the Diocesan Office set up in Buenos Aires three years ago, and the work of the Missions to Seamen and the Women's Diocesan Association.[8]

He then turned his attention to world affairs in a time of war. Synod was meeting in the depressing period after the Japanese had entered the war and achieved early successes, but just before the tide of German advances was turned by the victory at El Alamein. So he warned his hearers that defeatism was an ever-present danger against which the Christian raises the most emphatic of protests. He recalled the great faith which had overcome dangers, difficulties, trials and temptations faced by

---

[5] Report in local press.
[6] Ibid.
[7] Ibid.
[8] Ibid.

many outstanding figures of English history, and exhorted his hearers to strive for the same invincible faith.

Synods, however, are concerned not just with world affairs, but with mundane domestic matters, and its members turned their attention to the matter of fundraising and which methods were and were not allowable for a Christian church. A motion was introduced asserting that 'direct giving was the only way of raising Church funds', and Jack made an 'inspired speech' in support of it. 'Why is the world at war? Because it wants to get and not to give [...] Christ gave [...] There is only one way to raise money for the Church [...] We must teach mankind to give.'

In spite of Jack's eloquence, the motion was defeated. A long debate followed, with much discussion about whether raffles were a form of gambling, and in the end, in true Anglican fashion, a compromise motion was passed. It affirmed that direct giving was the only true method of raising money, but recognised that there were other ways of doing so, and 'discountenanced any methods involving gambling in any shape or form.'[9]

---

[9] Ibid.

Araucania, the North-West and Chaco 1942–3

Soon after Synod ended, Elisabeth made her first flight, accompanying her parents across the Andes, where her father had important business on the west coast. There were confirmations of twenty-nine candidates in Valparaíso and twenty-seven in Santiago,[1] then the family travelled to Temuco, the centre of the Araucanian mission. As he travelled around the Mission District (much of which he had to do on horseback, as there was a shortage of fuel),[2] Jack was encouraged to find that much of the evangelistic and educational work was now being done by Araucanian converts themselves. There were schools scattered around the country mainly run by ex-pupils of the Mission,[3] and there was a body called the Native Araucanian Missionary Society, a meeting of which Jack attended. 'Although I could not understand all the speeches,' he wrote, 'I gathered from among those present there was a spirit of enthusiasm and desire to bring the people to know Christ. Many of those present had ridden tremendous distances, starting hours before daylight, in order to be there.'[4] The Revd Juan Antinao, the only Araucanian priest, and Segundo Cayul, who was just about to be ordained, spoke 'well and forcefully' about the Christian life, making good use of their Bibles. Jack described the two men as 'natural leaders of the meeting.'[5]

Cayul's ordination itself took place on the Sunday before Christmas. He had received instruction from Canon Wilson, and had done well in the examination that it was necessary to pass before he could be admitted to the priesthood. His answers to the questions he had been set were shown to Jack, who was agreeably

---

[1] *Our Diocese*, June 1943.
[2] Report in *The Herald*, Buenos Aires.
[3] *Our Diocese*, June 1943.
[4] Ibid.
[5] *SAMS Magazine*, May–June 1943.

surprised at the progress Cayul had made. Juan Antinao was the preacher at the service, speaking 'very much to the point in Spanish', and Cayul was 'overjoyed at being priested'. Jack added, 'I have great hopes of his ministry.'[6]

The Christmas services were well attended, and there was a large congregation on the following Sunday when there was a Confirmation service at Cautinche, where Antinao lived and worked. Jack gave the address in Spanish, and Antinao repeated the substance in Mapudungu, the local language. 'After the service,' Jack wrote, 'we had a delightful picnic for the staff in a pleasant dell on Juan Antinao's land. Both he and Cayul were with us, and it was a pleasure to see them mix so happily and naturally with the English staff.'[7] The devoted work of the missionaries, supported by Jack in recent years, was clearly bearing fruit with the emergence of a strong local church.

Jack's next task was to make an extended tour of the northern parts of the Church's work on the western side of the continent, so he left Frances and Elisabeth with the Revd and Mrs K. M Howell at Quepe, the Mission's headquarters. As the weather warmed up at the end of the year, the Howells took them to Pichilemu, a coastal resort south of Valparaíso.

Jack's first stop was at Concepción, another coastal resort, where the church had been badly damaged in the earthquake. He confirmed ten candidates in a chapel which had been set up in the local school hall; this was a temporary arrangement while a permanent dual-purpose church and hall was under construction. There was no priest at Concepción, but a layman took services regularly and Canon Wilson came down from the Mission to celebrate communion once a month. After two days there, Jack went by train to Santiago, where he had twenty-four hours to obtain the tickets and documents he needed before flying 1,730 miles northwards to Lima.

The Church of the Good Shepherd in Lima was built in days when denominations other than Roman Catholic were not allowed to put up a building that looked like a church. From the outside it looked like an ordinary house, but inside it was in fact

---

[6] Ibid.
[7] *Our Diocese*, June 1943.

an excellent church. Jack confirmed seventeen candidates there and then flew to the oilfields of Northern Peru.[8] There had been no clergyman in that area since his last visit three years previously, so there were a good many baptisms to perform as well as celebrations of communion. 'You can imagine what it means to these communities,' he wrote, 'when the opportunity does come (once in three years) for corporate worship and communion.'[9]

Jack now made a short flight to Guayaquil in Ecuador, where he baptised three babies, then went back by rail to Ancon in Peru, where there were more baptisms. He also conducted a communion service there, and this, too, was the first for three years and much appreciated. After this he returned to Guayaquil and then flew first to Lima, where he confirmed four more adults, and then to La Paz, the capital of Bolivia.

Jack was now in the district where the Anglican churches had since 1936 been served by Canon A J K Thompson, who lived at Antofagasta on the coast. This meant that the Canon was frequently travelling great distances to minister to scattered congregations, situated anywhere from sea level to 14,000 feet. Three years earlier, Jack had tried to persuade him to give up this strenuous task, for he was not a young man, but he refused to leave until, not surprisingly, his health broke down. After months in hospital, he was eventually well enough to be taken by Jack to Buenos Aires and placed on a vessel to England. The ship was torpedoed 500 miles short of its destination, and the Canon died of injuries he received, and was buried at sea.[10]

Jack now visited many of the congregations previously served by Canon Thompson, ending in Antofagasta, where the community was further saddened when he had to tell them he did not know when they would next have a resident chaplain, or even a visit from one.

Jack's northern tour was now finished. He commented, 'The pace towards the end was really too rapid. In the last eight days I had visited five places, hundreds of miles apart, five journeys by plane, eleven services, five receptions, three Committee meetings

---

[8] Ibid.
[9] Ibid.
[10] Ibid.

and many social engagements. These with the change of altitude from sea-level to 14,000 feet were more than is good for the human frame and next time, this part of the programme must be done at a more leisurely pace.'[11]

Jack was now reunited with Frances and Elisabeth, and they returned to Buenos Aires, where a reporter of the *Standard* quoted the bishop as saying 'We are all very fit – especially Miss Elisabeth.' However, Jack was not able to rest for long. Having visited the Araucanians at the start of his recent trip, he was now due to visit the other main mission district where the South American Missionary Society was at work. This was among the Chaco, and now Jack had the satisfaction of licensing the first member of this tribe to be a lay reader. He arrived at Makthlawaiya Mission in Paraguay by plane, which was the first time this had been done, involving a flight of an hour and ten minutes from Asunción, the Paraguayan capital, instead of the normal four or five days by cart.[12] Besides licensing Augustine, the new reader, Jack baptised two people and confirmed three – events which, one of the missionaries, F Train, remarked, 'consolidate the normal advance of a young Church, increasing the membership and extending the evangelisation of other tribes'.[13]

Jack stayed for seventeen days altogether at the Mission, which enabled him to conduct services in Holy Week. Train ended his account of Jack's visit by writing,

> We remember with gratitude the quiet time in church on Good Friday – the message Bishop Weller left with us, the Communion services for the Indians and staff – and, with sorrow, the hurried departure – the plane came a day earlier than expected […] Looking back we thank God for the episcopal visit of Bishop Weller, praise God for all the blessings received.[14]

---

[11] Ibid.
[12] *SAMS Magazine*, Nov–Dec, 1943.
[13] Ibid.
[14] Ibid.

Last Years in the Diocese 1943–1946

By 1944, the diocese was again in need of more staff, and Jack decided to seek the necessary recruits in England and to take the opportunity to participate in the centenary celebrations of the South American Missionary Society. The first stage of the journey was in an Argentine ship bound for New Orleans. The journey was a long one, because the vessel was diverted to Cristobal, at the entrance to the Panama Canal. There, Jack again met Bishop Beal, who asked him to preach in the local church on the Sunday evening they were in port. The custom at that time was for white people to worship in the morning and coloured ones in the evening, so Jack found himself preaching to a sea of black and brown faces, and two white ones – Frances and Elisabeth.

On landing in New Orleans, they went by train to New York, and stayed for a few days with Jack's brother Morton in Schenectady. For the Atlantic crossing, they embarked on a liner which had been converted to transport large numbers, and they travelled in some discomfort as part of a convoy of fifty ships, landing with some relief at Liverpool. Their privations did not end there, for wartime conditions were something of a shock, especially to three-year-old Elisabeth, who on a visit to Fullers complained to her father that there was no soap, towel or lavatory paper in the toilet, and she wanted to go back to New York.

The Missionary Society would have liked to arrange a meeting in London to welcome Jack, but this was a time when flying bombs made people reluctant to visit the capital, so alternative arrangements had to be made.[1]

Jack succeeded in finding the clergy he needed to fill the vacant chaplaincies in his diocese, but he did not himself go back immediately, because he and Frances were looking forward to the arrival of another baby. Their son John was born in March, 1945.

---

[1] Minutes of the General Committee of the SAMS, 23/08/44.

Last Years in the Diocese 1943–1946

Jack had now completed eleven years as bishop of his enormous diocese, travelling vast distances to visit the various chaplaincies and missions. He and Frances now felt that 'the job was no longer suitable for a married man with a family', so he decided to settle in England after one final visit to the diocese.[2]

He went first to the Falklands, and had the usual difficulty in getting a passage from there to the mainland until the Navy came to his rescue with a minesweeper, which took him to Punta Arenas in the extreme south. From there he covered practically the whole of the diocese, involving journeys of many thousands of miles, before leaving by air for New York, and then England.

Perhaps the best summary of Jack's work in South America was provided by the Revd B A Tompkins, who wrote in the Journal of the South American Missionary Society as follows:

> I first met him in 1939 when he was translated from the Diocese of Falkland Islands to the Anglican Diocese in Argentina and Eastern South America, succeeding Bishop Every who had been its bishop for thirty-five years. It was not easy to take over from one who had served so long and was greatly loved by his people; but John R Weller was a man who had the gifts required to enter upon such a situation, and by his humility, his integrity, his love for his fellow men and, above all, his dependence upon God, he soon won the loyalty and affection of the people of the eastern diocese.
>
> At this time he became General Superintendent of the SAMS missions. He loved to visit the missions and on more than one occasion expressed regret that he was unable to spend more time with the missionaries and the Indians.
>
> He was truly a man of God and a man of prayer. It was my privilege to accompany him on a number of occasions on tours of the missions in Northern Argentina. Often this would involve camping out under the stars for a night or two. On these occasions the Bishop would rise early and go out into the forest for prayer and meditation before starting out on the next stretch of the tour. On the missions he would always endeavour to minister to the primitive people in their own languages as far as he could, spending hours in learning parts of the services in the native tongues.

---

[2] Weller, J R, *Bishop over the Andes*.

Last Years in the Diocese 1943–1946

It was a sad day for the Church in South America when, in 1945, the Bishop was called to return to England, and there are, I am sure, many missionaries who were privileged to serve under him who would join me in saying: 'I thank God in all my remembrances of him; thankful for his partnership in the Gospel over eight difficult years.'[3]

---

[3] Journal of SAMS, March–April 1970.

Edwalton and Holme Pierrepont 1946–58

Jack was now sixty-five years old, which is the age at which many clergymen retire, but this was something he had no intention of doing. His brother Chris had served in the Diocese of Southwell (now Southwell and Nottingham) for many years, and Jack joined him there. He was appointed to be Assistant Bishop in the diocese, and to be Vicar of Edwalton, which was then a mainly rural parish just across the Trent from the City of Nottingham. Jack's career up to this time had been an exceptional one; from now on it was more conventional, apart from the advanced age at which he undertook his new responsibilities. For this reason, the story of the remaining years of his life can be told more briefly.

Early in 1946, Jack, Frances and their two children moved into the Old House in Village Street, Edwalton, which had been the Vicarage since the 1880s. Jack told a reporter from the Nottingham Journal that 'he had come from South America to Southwell with one ambition ... to settle down with his wife and small son and daughter in a home of his own.'

The institution was performed by the Bishop of Southwell, Russell Barry, who remarked that this was the first time he had ever instituted a brother bishop to a parish. He warned that Jack's duties as Assistant Bishop would quite often take him away from the parish, and he added that he supposed that in fifty or one hundred years' time, Edwalton would be standing in the centre of a big suburb with a very large population around it; he was right, apart from his vast overestimation of the time-scale.

Jack now settled down to the work of an incumbent, serving a parish that still contained four working farms within half a mile of the much-loved Church of the Holy Rood. The Vicarage had a fair-sized garden, which Jack much enjoyed tending, usually wearing his oldest clothes. On one occasion a passer-by, seeing him expertly using a scythe, expressed the hope that the vicar was paying him properly for his labours.

Edwalton and Holme Pierrepont 1946-58

Jack at his institution as Vicar of Edwalton by Bishop Barry of Southwell, with Archdeacon Wilson and the two churchwardens, Messrs Booth and Herring in attendance.

Jack's help in the diocese was much appreciated by Bishop Barry, who wrote, 'We secured that gallant man, John Weller, retired from his arduous diocese in the Falkland Islands, who was in all sorts of ways a strong support to me.'[1]

What Jack described as 'the climax of my ministerial career' occurred in 1948, when the Lambeth Conference, postponed from 1940, finally took place. During the three weeks that preceded the actual Conference, teams of bishops visited dioceses around the country, speaking of their work. This meant that life for a time reverted to its old tempo, with constant travelling, speaking in churches, schools or factories, and numerous social engagements. Jack much enjoyed the companionship of the bishops who travelled with him, and was greatly encouraged by the interest shown by the various audiences whom they addressed.

---

[1] Barry, *Period of My Life*, Hodder & Stoughton, London, 1970, p.168.

At the Conference itself, Jack found himself mingling with bishops 'of different colour, black bishops, brown bishops, yellow bishops, bishops who had served in the forces, bishops who had suffered in concentration camps, American and Australian bishops – men with a single inflexible purpose in mind – the extension of the Kingdom of God.' They worked hard and produced a report which was translated into many languages, encouraging the faithful in many lands with the confident assertion that 'the Church lives in the power of the resurrection.'

There was also a considerable amount of social activity. The wives had their own meetings, and husbands and wives together were entertained at the Mansion House, the Houses of Parliament and Buckingham Palace. At a reception in the garden of the Palace, the King, Queen and other members of the royal family shook hands with all the bishops. One large black lady had become separated from her husband, so Jack and Frances made room for her next to them.[2] The story goes that Mary the Queen Mother assumed it was she who was Jack's wife.

By the late 1940s, it was clear that the population of Edwalton would soon increase dramatically, as the post-war housing boom turned it into a suburb of Nottingham. This meant it was no longer an appointment which could be combined with that of an assistant bishop, so in 1949 Jack moved a few miles farther from the city to become Rector of the rural parish of Holme Pierrepont.

There are many memories of his time in that parish. 'He was always available to everyone, however tired he was or whoever they were,' writes his daughter. A parishioner remarks on the fact that he joined in everything, including the cleaning of the church. Two students at Nottingham University who lodged in the Rectory remember it as a place where there was much laughter; 'We had the opportunity to develop our senses of humour,' writes one of them. A man who grew up in the parish remembers with gratitude the way Jack conducted assemblies at the Church School. There was one occasion when the car was not available for him to drive to the school, so he accepted the invitation to ride on the pillion of an old 'Ambassador' motorcycle belonging to

---

[2] Ibid, p.175.

one of the student lodgers. He thought this was great fun, but Frances was horrified when she heard about it. One permanent reminder of his time in the parish is provided by the altar rails, which he donated in memory of Alexina.

Jack spent a good deal of time in the Rectory garden, providing practically all the vegetables and fruit needed by the household; he also reared pigs in it. As in Edwalton, when working there he always wore his gardening clothes – an ancient shirt, a disreputable cardigan, and trousers which, it is said, were held up with Frances' stockings. On one occasion, a well-dressed clergyman called and, mistaking Jack for the gardener, said, 'My good man, is the bishop at home?' Jack, with his impish sense of humour, assured the visitor that the bishop was indeed at home and that he would fetch him. A few minutes later, he reappeared, dressed as a bishop.

The garden had another use besides the production of fruit, vegetables and bacon. There was one special path where, when Jack was walking up and down it, the family knew he must not be disturbed. He was continuing the practice of prayer and meditation which had been a feature of his devotional life throughout his ministry.

The years at Holme Pierrepont were ones when the children were growing up. His son John, who was born when Jack was sixty-four, never felt that the age gap mattered, as his father had a remarkable ability to communicate across the generations. His daughter Elisabeth remarks on the interest he showed in all that she and John were doing, and that he played billiards with them in the winter, and table tennis, at which he was not so good, in the summer. He did not find it necessary to be a strict disciplinarian, as his example showed his children how to behave.

In 1952, Bishop Barry spent some time in the USA on a Sabbatical. He returned to find that 'Bishop Weller and the two archdeacons had looked after the diocese so well that it had taken no harm through my absence. Indeed it seemed to have got on rather better.'[3]

Although he was Rector of a country parish, Jack was well aware of the needs of industry, and he frequently visited factories

---

[3] Weller, J R, *Bishop over the Andes*.

in urban areas. These included not just the major Nottingham ones – Boots, Raleigh and Viyella – but often ones farther afield. On many of these occasions he took Elisabeth and John with him.[4]

In 1958, at the age of seventy-nine, Jack finally ceased to be responsible for a parish.

---

[4] The author is grateful to all those who have shared memories of Jack's time in the two Nottinghamshire parishes – especially Mrs Elisabeth O'Gorman (his daughter), Brigadier John Weller, Canon Brian Beaumont, Mr Godfrey Hare and Mrs Ellen Meredith.

The Final Years 1958–1969[1]

Jack and Frances now moved to accommodation for retired clergy in Newland, just outside Malvern, Worcestershire. 'Retired', however, does not describe Jack's situation. He became an assistant bishop in Worcester Diocese, and in that capacity not only conducted Confirmation services in many parts of the county, but in times when parishes were without an incumbent, he would take the Sunday services until the new vicar was instituted. St John's, Worcester and the village church in Wichenford were ones in which he did stints of two or three months in that way.

Jack also remained physically active. He was granted an allotment in the garden of the Newland vicarage, which gave him opportunities for an activity he had always enjoyed. On his eighty-fifth birthday in 1965, he climbed to the highest point of the Malvern Hills: the Worcestershire Beacon. Earlier in that year, Elisabeth, who had emigrated to Australia, was getting married, and Jack hoped to fly out there for the occasion, but the doctor forbade him to do so. On the day itself, he and Frances were staying with a former lodger from Holme Pierrepont days, who was now the vicar of St Alban's, Smethwick, a parish in the West Midlands. They and their host prayed for the young couple in the church.

Jack interpreted the doctor's prohibition as applying only to air travel, so in the following year he used a form of transport that he had employed often in the past, booking a berth on a cargo boat. This enabled him and Frances to visit Elisabeth and her husband at the time their first child was born.

In the evening of 27 October 1969, Jack conducted a Confirmation service at St Leonard's, Newland. There were fourteen candidates; boys from Malvern College, girls who had been prepared by the Sisters from Holy Name Convent, which was still that community's Mother House. Jack came home and

---
[1] Information for this chapter supplied by Brigadier J P Weller.

had supper, and since he had, as always, put a lot into the service he had conducted, he felt the need to rest, and settled down in an armchair with a glass of whisky. A few minutes later, he died.

Fortunately for Frances, their son John, in the earlier stages of his distinguished army career, had returned home two days previously, after a six-month posting in Cyprus. He was able to support his mother in the days that followed. The funeral was at St Leonard's, Newland, and Jack was buried in the churchyard. Frances survived him by twenty-three years and is buried in the same grave.

The obituary in *The Times* consisted of only a few lines listing his episcopal appointments, and that in the *Church Times* was also just a list of the offices he had held. It was left to the Newland parish newsletter to be rather more informative:

> No one who was present at the Confirmation will ever forget that unique occasion. It was not just another Confirmation; it was the last Episcopal act of Bishop Weller, as far as this life is concerned, and it was a triumphant conclusion to a long and varied ministry in the Church at home and overseas...
>
> Countless people in various parts of the world will have had good reason to be grateful for his ministry. For the past twelve years he had lived in Newland in happy and active retirement, beloved by all who knew him. His valuable help in the services here, in a voice that remained strong to the last, will be remembered with great gratitude, as he himself will be remembered with great affection.
>
> While we offer Mrs Weller and her family our sincere sympathy, we also join with them in thanksgiving to Almighty God for the pleasure and privilege of having known Bishop Weller, and for his great contribution to the life of this parish and community. May he rest in peace.

In his years in South America he made an enormous contribution to the subsequent spectacular growth of the Anglican Church in that continent, and the secret behind it is best summarised by a sentence, already quoted, written by the Revd B A Tompkins, with whom he had worked for so many years among the Chaco: 'he was truly a man of God and a man of prayer.'[2]

---

[2] Journal of SAMS, March–April 1970.

A Note on Sources

Unpublished

Bishop over the Andes was written by Bishop Weller in 1948–9. The typescript is in the possession of his son, Brigadier J P Weller.

A Few Notes Concerning the Edward Wellers was written by Canon C H Weller, also in 1948–9. The notes about each of the various members of this branch of the family are reproduced in the 'Weller Family Tree' website (www weller.org.uk). See under 'biographies' in the 'genealogical tree' section.

The Diary of J R Weller Sept 1934–April 1935. This is the only surviving part of his diary, consisting of handwritten transcripts in the possession of the present writer.

Untitled. A four-page manuscript by Bishop Weller describing his journey from Mendoza to Buenos Aires on his way back from Chile in March, 1939, in the possession of the present writer.

Reports to the Archbishop of Canterbury. Bishop Weller's reports, addressed to Canon McCloud Campbell of the Church Assembly Missionary Council, are in the Lambeth Palace Library.

Published

South American Missionary Society Magazine

Mersey Missions to Seamen 1856–1956

Thanks are due respectively to Mr R Lunt and Ms A Haines for photocopies of relevant extracts from the above periodicals.

Use has been made of many cuttings from Buenos Aires newspapers in the possession of Brigadier Weller. There are no dates or names of the papers attached, so it has not been possible to provide detailed footnotes.

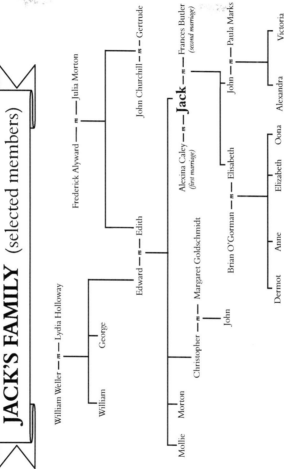

The REVD JOHN WELLER MA BD is the eldest son of Jack's brother Chris. He was ordained in 1952, and his ministry in the next thirty-eight years was divided almost equally between parishes in the English Midlands, and the Province of Central Africa. He was Warden of St John's Seminary Lusaka for seven years, and his last appointment in full-time ministry was as Rector of Harare Cathedral. He and his wife Jean now live in retirement in Bristol. Their elder son, the Revd David Weller, is currently chaplain to the English-speaking community in Rio de Janeiro – and so ministers to a congregation which once formed part of his great-uncle's diocese.

Previous publications

The Priest from the Lakeside (The Life of Leonard Kamungu of Malawi and Zambia), CLAIM, Malawi, 1971

Themes in the Christian History of Central Africa, Heinemann, London, 1975 (Edited with Prof. T Ranger)

Mainstream Christianity to 1980 in Malawi, Zambia and Zimbabwe, Mambo Press, Zimbabwe, 1984 (with Jane Linden)

Index

—A—

Afghanistan, 23
Allenby, General E H H, 23
Amersham, Bucks, 11, 12
Andrews, Revd C F, 20, 21
Antinao, the Revd Juan, 49, 57, 74
Antofagasta, Chile, 41, 50, 67, 68, 76
Araucanians, 36–37, 48–49, 50, 57, 60, 77
Arequipa, Peru, 41, 67
Argentina
  Buenos Aires, 25, 33, 38, 40, 41, 44, 49, 50, 53, 54, 58, 59, 62, 65, 70, 71, 72, 76, 77, 88
  Trelew, 59, 64
Asunción, Paraguay, 62, 77
Australia
  Melbourne, 25, 26, 28, 38, 40, 56
  Tasmania, 26
Aylward, the Revd A F, 11

—B—

Barry, Bishop Russell, 81, 82, 84
Beal, Bishop, 69, 78
Bogotá, Colombia, 69
Bolivia
  La Paz, 42, 67, 68, 76
Brazil
  Rio de Janeiro, 44, 54, 92
Britain
  Amersham, Bucks, 11, 12
  Cambridge, 19, 20
    Girton College, 21
    Selwyn College, 19, 20, 21
  Dordon, Warwickshire, 25
  Edwalton, Notts, 81, 82, 83, 84
  Greenwich, London
    Christ Church, 25
  Holme Pierrepont, Notts, 83, 84, 86
  Liverpool, 16, 27, 31, 38, 78
  Newland, Worcestershire, 86, 87
    St Leonard's Church, 86
  Nottingham, 81, 83, 85
Brooke, Miss, 38
Buenos Aires, Argentina, 25, 33, 38, 40, 41, 44, 49, 50, 53, 54, 58, 59, 62, 65, 70, 71, 72, 76, 77, 88
Butler, Frances. *See* Frances Weller

Index

—C—
Caley, Alexina. *See* Alexina Weller
Cambridge Mission to Delhi, 20, 21
Cape Town, South Africa, 16, 26
Cayul, the Revd Segundo, 57, 74, 75
Ceylon, now Sri Lanka, 14, 16, 20, 24
Chicago, USA, 17
Chile
  Antofagasta, 41, 50, 67, 68, 76
  Iquique, 42, 67
  Magellanes, 38, 40, 49
  Punta Arenas, 43, 65, 79
  Santiago, 35, 40, 41, 50, 51, 58, 59, 65, 74, 75
  Temuco, 36, 38, 50, 74
  Tolten, 36, 48
  Valparaíso, 33, 34, 35, 38, 41, 43, 47, 48, 49, 50, 51, 65, 74, 75
    St Paul's Church, 34, 35
    St Peter's Church, 34
Colombia
  Bogotá, 69
—D—
Damascus, Syria, 23
Delhi
  Cambridge Mission to, 20
Delhi, India, 21, 23
Dordon, Warwickshire, 25
—E—
Ecuador
  Guayaquil, 76
Emery, the Revd Stanley, 19
Evans, Bishop J, 63, 66, 71
Every, Bishop J, 43, 49, 79
—F—
Falkland Islands, 30, 33, 41, 47, 48, 49, 50, 51, 65, 72, 79, 82
  Port Stanley, 30, 38, 39, 40
—G—
Greenwich, London, 25
Guayaquil, Ecuador, 76
Gwalior, India, 22
—H—
Hindenburg, 44, 45
—I—
India
  Delhi, 21, 23
  Gwalior, 22
  Karachi, 23
  Taj Mahal, 22
Iquique, Chile, 42, 67
Israel
  Jerusalem, 23
—J—
Jerusalem, Israel, 23
—K—
Karachi, India (now Pakistan), 23
Kipling, Mr Percy, 53
—L—
La Paz, Bolivia, 42, 67, 68, 76
Lambeth Conference, 1948, 82
Lang, Archbishop Cosmo, 30, 31, 63, 70, 72

Index

Lima, Peru, 32, 41, 68, 69, 75, 76
Liverpool, Britain, 16, 27, 31, 38, 78
—M—
Magellan, Straits of, 33, 38, 43
Magellanes, Chile, 38, 40, 49
Mapuche. *See* Araucanians
Language, 37
Melbourne, Australia, 25, 26, 28, 38, 40, 56
Michell, Keith, 35
Michell, Mollie née Weller, 35
Michell, Sir Robert and Lady, 35
Missions to Seamen (now Mission to Seafarers), 25–29, 33, 34, 56, 71, 72
Montevideo, Uruguay, 33, 40
—N—
New York, USA, 19, 31, 46, 47, 70, 78, 79
Newland, Worcestershire, 86, 87
   St Leonard's Church, 86, 87
Nottingham, Britain, 81, 83, 85
—O—
O'Gorman, Mrs Elisabeth, née Weller, 71, 74, 75, 77, 78, 84, 85, 86
—P—
Pakistan
   Karachi. *See* India
Panama, 7, 30, 32, 33, 64, 69, 70, 78
Paraguay
   Asunción, 62, 77
   Chaco, area, 69
   Chaco, people, 60, 77, 87
Peru
   Arequipa, 41
   Lima, 32, 41, 68, 69, 75, 76
Port Stanley, Falkland Islands, 30, 38, 39, 40
Punta Arenas, Chile, 43, 65, 79
—R—
Rio de Janeiro, Brazil, 44, 54, 92
—S—
SAMS. *See* South American Missionary Society
Santiago de Compostela, Spain, 32
Santiago, Chile, 35, 40, 41, 50, 51, 58, 59, 65, 74, 75
Selwyn College, Cambridge, 19, 20, 21
South Africa
   Cape Town, 16, 26
South American Missionary Society, 36, 51, 60, 71, 77, 78, 79, 88
South Georgia, island of, 7, 30, 39
Spain
   Santiago de Compostela, 32
Sri Lanka. *See* Ceylon

95

Index

St George's Cathedral,
  Jerusalem, 23
St Leonard's Church
  Newland, 86, 87
St Paul's Church
  Concord, New
    Hampshire, 19
  Valparaíso, Chile, 34, 35
St Peter's Church
  Valparaíso, Chile, 34
Syria
  Damascus, 23

—T—

Taj Mahal, India, 22
Tasmania, Australia, 26
Temple, Archbishop
  William, 72
Temuco, Chile, 36, 38, 50, 74
Thompson, Canon A J K, 76
Tolten, Chile, 36, 48
Tompkins, the Revd B A, 60, 61, 62, 79, 87
Townsend, Canon, 71
Train, the Revd F, 77
Trelew, Argentina, 59, 64

—U—

Uruguay
  Montevideo, 33, 40
USA
  Chicago, 17
  Concord, New
    Hampshire, 17, 20
      St Paul's Church, 18, 19
  St Paul's School, 19
  New York, 19, 31, 46, 47, 70, 78, 79

—V—

Valparaíso, Chile, 33, 34, 35, 38, 41, 43, 47, 48, 49, 50, 51, 65, 74, 75
  St Peter's Church, 34

—W—

Weller
  Alexina, née Caley, 21, 23, 25, 26, 27, 28, 30, 31, 53, 84
  Brigadier John, 78, 84, 85, 87
  Canon Christopher, 13, 25, 31, 88
  Edith, née Aylward, 11, 12, 13
  Edward, 11, 12
  Elisabeth. *See* O'Gorman
  Frances, née Butler, 53, 54, 56, 58, 59, 60, 61, 62, 64, 65, 67, 68, 69, 70, 71, 75, 77, 78, 79, 81, 83, 84, 86, 87
  George, 11
  the Revd Morton, 16, 31, 47, 78
  William (b. 1727), 11
  William (b.1840), 11
Whaling, Archdeacon Foley, 32, 41
Wilson, Canon, 36, 37, 48, 74, 75

Printed in Great Britain
by Amazon